Hippocrene Great Religions of the World

THE
METHODISTS

James Haskins

HIPPOCRENE BOOKS
New York

To Louise

Acknowledgments

I wish to express my gratitude to the Wesleyan University Library, Wesleyan University, Middletown, Connecticut, for providing access to their extensive collection on Methodism and Methodist history.

A special thank you to Anne Jordan.

Copyright © 1992 by James Haskins.

For information, contact:
HIPPOCRENE BOOKS, INC.
171 Madison Avenue
New York, NY 10016

ISBN 0-7818-0029-3

Printed in the United States of America

Library of Congress Cataloging-in-Publication data

Haskins, James, 1941-
  The Methodists / James Haskins.
    p   cm. — (Hippocrene great religions of the world)
  Includes bibliographical references and index.
  ISBN 0-7818-0029-3 (cloth) : 14.95
  1. Methodist Church   2. Methodist Church—United
States.   3. United Methodist Church (U.S.)   I. Title.   II. Series.
BX8331.2.h42   1992
287—dc20   92-28906
                                                    CIP

Contents

Preface

METHODISM IS A FORM OF CHRISTIANITY THAT HAS RE-
curred throughout history but which was given defini-
tion and permanency by John and Charles Wesley
during the eighteenth century. Initially a group of "societies" within the Church of England, Methodism became a separate denomination when the bishop of
London refused to ordain ministers to serve the Methodists in England and America.

One of the chief beliefs of the Methodists is that
"doctrine which is not proved in devotion and life and
does not issue in practical charity is useless."[1] One
should live a life of faith, and that faith should show
itself in the form of good works. Under the guidance of
John and Charles Wesley, early members of the church
followed a strict daily schedule of charitable and religious activities, and charity toward others has continued to be a strong pillar of the Methodist Church.

The Methodists also believe in the Holy Trinity, a
conscious fellowship with God, and a church order in
which the laity stand alongside—rather than beneath—
the clergy. The church is Arminian rather than fully
Calvinistic in its beliefs, opposing the idea of pre-

destination and upholding belief in the salvation of all who have been "justified" by faith.

Methodism as a denomination can be said to have formally originated on June 25, 1744, when its first conference was held in London, led by John and Charles Wesley. The Methodist Church in America was organized some years later in Baltimore on December 24, 1784. On April 22, 1968, the Methodist Church and the Evangelical United Brethren Church joined together to become the United Methodist Church, as it is still known today.

The United Methodists follow three books: the Bible, which is, naturally, of greatest importance; the *Book of Hymns*; and the Books of Discipline, collections of covenants agreed upon by the members of the church. The United Methodists recognize only two sacraments as holy: baptism and the Lord's Supper (Holy Communion). Marriage and confirmation are revered, but not viewed as sacraments; only those rites performed by Christ are deemed to be sacraments.

The Methodist attitudes toward charity and social responsibility are only two factors that make the denomination distinctive. The church has long been a leader in these areas. Another characteristic that defines Methodism is what John Wesley called "the witness of the spirit." This is "an inward impression on the soul whereby the spirit of God immediately and directly witnesses to my spirit that I am a child of God . . . that all my sins are blotted out and I am reconciled to God."[2] Because of this, Methodists have emphasized conversion, revivals, and testimonies of religious experiences.

Methodism started as a small "Holy Club" organized

by John and Charles Wesley at Oxford University. It has now spread world wide in a loosely connected fellowship of Churches, bound together by the World Methodist Council. Today the Methodist Church has over ten million members in the United States alone, twenty million world wide, and is growing daily.

I

"The Best of Times, The Worst of Times"

EIGHTEENTH-CENTURY ENGLAND WAS A STRIKING STUDY in contrasts as it moved into the age of industrialization. Charles Dickens described it, nearly a century later, as "the best of times . . . the worst of times." Dotting the green and gently rolling countryside were the great estates of the wealthy; nearby were the squalid cottages of the laborers who supported them. Noble houses afforded the gentry a life filled with ease. Their libraries held the latest books, their galleries were hung with the finest artwork. But while lords and their ladies dined in comfort, laborers too often subsisted in poverty on bread, cheese, potatoes, and beer. What meat they had frequently was obtained illegally by poaching on the local lord's estate.

Too, while living on these estates was luxurious, getting to them was often a problem. The roads throughout England were in lamentable condition, so much so that Queen Anne once found that she could not travel from Bristol to nearby Bath because the road was virtually nonexistent.[1] In the early 1740s, Daniel Defoe wrote, "The Country indeed remains in the utmost distress for want of good roads." Arthur Young later noted—during the time when John Wesley was traveling as an itinerant preacher—"In all England there are but four good roads; the rest it would be a Prostitution of Language to call Turnpikes."[2] But change was coming.

At the start of the eighteenth century, England was largely rural, but as the century progressed, disgruntled agricultural workers were giving up plowing the land and moving to the suddenly growing towns and cities that held, for them, at least a slim chance of a better life. As machinery eased the labor of manufacture, towns and cities grew up centering around a particular trade. Leicester trade, for example, focused upon framework knitting; and Birmingham and surrounding towns turned to the production of hardware made from the ore of nearby iron mines.

The growth of these urban centers heralded the establishment of a trade class. Suddenly butchers and bakers and grocers were needed to supply goods to the laboring class. All were crammed into towns and cities then ill-equipped to accommodate them.

Of all the British cities and towns, London was pre-eminent, with over half a million people by the end of the eighteenth century. At the west end lay Westminster, the seat of goverment. Many in London devoted their lives to supplying its needs. But London was also a great port city, the busiest in England. Because there was almost no highway system, London not only carried on a bustling foreign trade, but also supplied smaller British ports with goods by water.

Although London was the largest and most magnificent city in England, it was also, for many, a wretched place in which to live. Merchants and wealthier shopkeepers lived comfortably for the times, but for the poor, London was a fetid place of criminality and disease. Lacking proper sanitation, London threw its garbage haphazardly into the streets, down the center of which sewage ran in open streams, providing a breeding ground for disease and pestilence. Crime was rampant: beneath the fashionable and cultured lives of the upper classes existed an "underworld of thieves, footpads, forgers, beggars, and harlots, sometimes as highly organized as the criminal area of Chicago at the most lurid point of its history."[3]

No matter how primitive life in the countryside was, life in the city was often worse. The average Londoner's life-span was shorter than that of the rural laborer. One contemporary, Gregory King, cited a five-fold cause for this: "More frequent Fornications & Adulteries . . . Greater Luxury & Intemperance . . . a Greater Intenseness of Businesse . . . the Unhealthfullnesse of the Coal Smoak . . . and a greater Inequality of age Between the Husbands & Wives."[3]

Regardless of specifics, the fact is that London had

not yet caught up with its rapid growth, nor had technology and science advanced enough to equate disease and short life-spans with overcrowding and filth. Life in the eighteenth century was too often similar to that in nature earlier described by Thomas Hobbes: poor, nasty, brutish, and short. It was not until the century was well advanced that the government and various religious organizations turned to the task of improving the lot of the poor.

The Church of England in the eighteenth century was a somewhat weak reed upon which to lean for help in this world. The separatist movements of the previous century had weakened it both internally and externally, although it continued to be the predominant—and official—denomination.

In the early part of the sixteenth century, King Henry VIII had separated the English church from the Roman Catholic Church after a long period of protest and agitation against what many felt was an unwarranted usurpation of authority by the pope.[5] Henry VIII utterly rejected the pope's claim to sovereignty over the entire church.

Since the Church of England patterned itself in structure on the Catholic Church—without a pope, of course—many were still dissatisfied, feeling that the changes made were not enough. Separatist movements sprang up, led by dissenters who sought to form their own denominations in the face of new laws making such movements illegal. The separatists were initially hounded out of England by the passage of a number of laws intended to make them conform to the Church of England. Perhaps the best-known of these groups were the Puritans who fled to the New World in 1620 aboard the *Mayflower.*

During the English civil wars and the Commonwealth period (1640–1660), dissenting groups gained some ground against discrimination. Many saw Oliver Cromwell's battle against the authority of the British monarchy as a religious as well as a civil fight. To their eyes, the monarchy, like the pope before, was intruding too deeply into religious affairs by placing restrictions upon the dissenters.

Although there still existed resentment among the dissenting groups, and between them and the Church of England, the Commonwealth period allowed the various groups to grow and establish themselves firmly. So much so that when the monarchy was restored in 1661, King Charles II agreed to enact several laws against them. Known as the Clarendon Code, "these laws prevented nonconformists from holding public office, attending universities, conducting services or preaching without a special license; and compelled all dissenters to attend Anglican services."[6] Those who refused to obey them were imprisoned, tortured, and sometimes executed. One of the most famous of these was John Bunyan (1628–1688), the author of *Pilgrim's Progress* (1678), who was arrested in 1660 for preaching without a license and imprisoned for the next twelve years.

It was not until the ascension to the throne of William of Orange and Mary in 1689, and the passage of the Act of Toleration, that the situation stabilized. Although the act did not grant full religious freedom to nonconforming sects, and inroads were made upon it by later rulers, it was a step toward the separation of church and state that would not be fully realized for nearly one hundred years.

By the beginning of the eighteenth century, then, the Church of England was in a somewhat disordered state. While still the "official" religion, it had suffered a bleed-off of members to dissenting groups, and internal strife was rampant. Wealthy and favored members of the clergy were given a number of thriving parishes—many of which they never even visited—to provide them with a comfortable living. Those not in favor, however, or of inferior social status, were granted parishes and livings that barely allowed them to feed themselves and their families.

Because of its unique position as a state religion, Anglicanism wielded a big stick. The church controlled education. For example, subscription to the Thirty-Nine Articles, the basic doctrinal statement of the church, was required for admission to Oxford or Cambridge universities. Similarly, the church was influential in the law-making process since its bishops sat in the House of Lords and were appointed by the government. In turn the government was ready to support the church by the passage of favorable laws and the enforcement of the collection of tithes, a portion of which went to the king.

The Church of England was meant to be "an institution with which the majority could identify."[7] Increasingly, however, the population was finding this difficult. Not only were the blemishes of the church becoming more apparent, but increasing literacy threatened its basic underpinnings. The Age of Enlightenment, with its lively questioning of authority and traditional beliefs, its stress upon reason rather than faith, upon this world rather than the next, was making inroads upon the authority of the church. More and more people were coming to believe, as the English philosopher John Locke stated, that a man should be "well-skilled in knowledge of material causes and effects of things in his power; directing his thought to the improvement of such arts and inventions, engines and utensils, as might best contribute to his continuance with conveniency and delight."[8] This philosophy of materialism and reason was at odds with the Church of England as Calvinistic doctrine of predestination.

Those within the church struggled to reconcile these new secular ideas with the religious. One result was the eventual distinction between "High Church" and "Low Church," and an increased emphasis on reason. But even these attempts to cope with a changing world still left a gap between the secular and the religious: a need for faith and zeal. Into that gap was to step a young man whose "methods" seemed to draw the two together. In time, his work led to the reluctant establishment of an entirely new denomination.

II

"A Brand Plucked Out of the Burning"

THE VILLAGE OF EPWORTH IN THE ENGLISH FENS WAS remote and barbarous, a poor parish indeed, and his assignment to it came as a blow to Samuel Wesley, a strict Anglican curate who had aspirations as a poet. He had received his post and a stipend of £200 a year, in fact, because of his poetry. He had composed a heroic poem on the life of Christ and dedicated it to William III's queen, Mary, who had rewarded him with the parish of Epworth and the living of Wroote.

During his thirty-nine years as rector of Epworth,

Wesley never lost the hope that his poetry would come to some powerful patron's attention and, recognized for his ability to "woo the muses," he would be removed from the parish he detested, perhaps once more to live in the rarified atmosphere of London. This was never to occur. Samuel Wesley and his wife, Susanna, with their nine children, spent their years making their home a cultural island in the midst of a town filled with illiteracy and a distrust of the "airs" that he assumed. Samuel was isolated, remote, and heartily disliked in his own parish.

Both Samuel and Susanna came from backgrounds that prepared them for a life of sacrifice. Susanna was a beautiful and intelligent girl, the daughter of a Church of England minister, Dr. Samuel Annesley, who would become known as a nonconformist for his views against the church. Samuel Wesley's parents also had been dissenters, yet as he became older he was drawn more and more to the Church of England. Susanna, at the age of thirteen and despite her father's objections, had joined the church. When she later met the young curate, Samuel Wesley, she must have been drawn to him not only for his intellect but because he shared so similar a religious and familial defiance.

Samuel Wesley started his career as a curate in London and had great hopes not only for doing good works in and around that city, but also for gaining renown for his poetry. When he was only twenty-two years old, he published a volume entitled *Maggots* in the preface of which, under his own picture, he wrote,

In's own defence the Author writes
Because while this foul Maggot bites

He nere Can rest in quiet,
Which makes him make Soo sad a face
Heed beg your worship or your Grace
Seight unseen to buy it.

Maggots had moderate success, but was not the best-seller Samuel had hoped for.

When his next poem, on the life of Christ, brought him to the attention of Queen Mary, Samuel exulted, until he saw the reward his efforts had achieved for him: the parish of Epworth.

Epworth, in a remote part of Lincolnshire, lay to the south of the Isle of Axholme. During his years there, Samuel liked to refer to himself as the "Poet of the Isle of Axholme," or the "Island Poet," lofty titles little in keeping with the boggy tract of land bounded by rivers to which it referred. And in the isolation of Epworth, befriended almost solely by his family, Samuel's idiosyncrasies blossomed. Not only did he like the conceit of Island Poet, but also he "suffered from violent delusions, an uneasy temper, improvidence in worldly things, and an aggressively rigorous attitude to Anglicanism."[1]

This latter stance, coupled with the cultured airs which he assumed, made his parishioners openly hostile. Strict in requiring church attendance, Samuel also forced many to do penance by standing barefoot in the church aisle. His parishioners, in turn, mocked him and his children, joking about his pretensions and his inept management of the glebe lands given him (land whose farming provided partial support for the rector). Their attacks frequently went beyond the verbal, and he several times found his cattle maimed and his fields burned. Increasingly, Samuel withdrew into life in the rectory, creating his own, separate world.

In 1701, however, even that world disappointed him. In his daily prayers with the family, he had been accustomed to saying one for King William III. One day he noticed that Susanna refused to say "Amen." Although she was as devout as Samuel, her political views were opposed to his, something that Samuel obviously was unaware of until then. He was incensed. "If we have two kings, Sukey," he declared, "we must have two beds," and he departed for London.[2]

Samuel did not return to Epworth until the following year, a difficult one for Susanna who had been left with little to live on and a flock of children to care for. Samuel came back only after the rectory was partially burned by one of his disgruntled parishioners. During the intervening time, King William had died and Samuel and Susanna were able to come to a reconciliation with one another. On June 17, 1703, Samuel's and Susanna's fifteenth child, John Benjamin Wesley, was born.

Altogether, Susanna bore nineteen children, only nine of whom survived infancy. John Benjamin's brother Charles, who would share most of his work through life, was born four years later, in 1707.

John's early childhood was a portrait in contrasts. Within the rectory, quiet study and peace reigned, directed by Susanna's firm hand; without, chaos seemed to prevail, at least during his first few years— mostly, due to Samuel. In 1705, Samuel promised his support in a general election to a Colonel Whichcott. When he discovered, however, that Whichcott was also supported by a number of dissenters, of whom Samuel heartily disapproved, he withdrew his support and voted for the church candidate. This enraged the local citizenry. The supporters of Whichcott kept him and his family awake night after night, blowing horns and pounding on pots and pans. The more influential among them went further, however, resorting to other means of revenge.

Samuel was terrible at managing money and, as a result, was frequently in debt. A relative of Colonel Whichcott's named Pindar took advantage of this and had Samuel arrested and jailed for a debt of £30. Resigned to his fate, Samuel said, "Now I am at rest in the haven where I long expected to be! A jail is paradise in comparison of the life I led before I came here." Jailed for three months, Samuel finally appealed for help to John Sharpe, archbishop of York and a privy councilor. The archbishop obtained Samuel's release, paid his debts, and raised donations to help the family.

Although it was obvious that he was shunned by the village, Samuel insisted on returning to Epworth after his release, against the advice of both his friends and the archbishop. "I confess I am not of that mind," he wrote, "because I may yet do some good here; and 'tis like a coward to desert my post when the enemy fire is thick upon me. They have only wounded me yet, and, I believe, can't kill me."

If Samuel couldn't be killed, it was not for lack of trying. In 1709 a fire of unknown origin burned the Epworth rectory to the ground. Susanna Wesley described the events of that evening:

> On Wednesday night, February 9th, between the hours of eleven and twelve, our house took fire; from what cause God only knows. It was discovered by some

sparks falling from the roof upon a bed where one of the children lay, and burning her feet. . . . Mr. Wesley was alarmed by a cry of "Fire!" in the street. . . . On opening his door he found the house full of smoke, and the roof was already burnt through. He immediately came to my room (I was very ill in a separate room). . . . Then he ran and burst open the nursery door and called to the maid to bring out the children. . . . She snatched up the youngest and bid the rest follow, which they did, except Jacky [John Wesley]. When we were got into the hall and saw . . . that the roof was on the point of falling, we concluded ourselves inevitably lost. . . . Mr. Wesley had such presence of mind as to think of the garden door, out of which he helped some of the children; the rest got out through the windows; I was not in a condition to climb [being pregnant]. . . . In this distress I besought our blessed Saviour to preserve me, if it were his will, from that death, and then waded through the fire, naked as I was, which did me no further harm than a little scorching of my hands and feet.

While Mr. Wesley was carrying the children into the garden, he heard the child in the nursery cry out miserably for help. . . . He several times attempted the stairs, then on fire, and found they would not bear his weight. Finding it was impossible to get near him, he gave him up for lost, and kneeling down, he commended his soul to God, and left him, as he thought, perishing in the flames.[3]

The child, John Wesley, was not lost, however. Later he wrote of the fire and of his rescue:

Seeing the room was very light, I called to the maid to take me up. But none answering, I put my head out the curtains, and saw streaks of fire on top of the room. I got up and ran to the door, but could get no further, all the floor beyond it being in a blaze. I then climbed up a chest that stood near a window. One in the yard saw me and proposed running to fetch a ladder. Another answered, "There will not be time; but lift a light man, and set him on my shoulders." They did so, and he took me out of the window. Just then the roof fell; but it fell inward, or we had all been crushed at once. When they brought me into the house where my father was, he cried out, "Come neighbors, let us kneel down! Let us give thanks to God! He has given me all my eight children: let the house go, I am rich enough!"[4]

Susanna, likewise, welcomed her son back into her arms, exclaiming, "Is this not a brand plucked out of the burning?" This phrase was to stay with John all his life and he later had it inscribed under one of his portraits. After this episode, although all her children were dear to her, Susanna felt that John was singled out and was meant for something special in life.

The following years were relatively quiet ones for Samuel Wesley and his family. Shocked by the fire, the parishioners refrained from any more physical attacks upon their rector, and Samuel returned to his writing, his passion. He continued, however, to ignore the more material aspects of life, and his family still found themselves forced to struggle for subsistence at times. But an uneasy peace reigned at Epworth; Samuel was reluctantly accepted as rector and he looked far to the future, expecting one of his sons to fill his "post" there after he died, little realizing how very different their mission in life would come to be.

III

Young John Wesley

"I INSIST," STATED SUSANNA WESLEY, "UPON CONQUERING the will of the children betimes because this is the only strong and rational foundation of a religious education." Susanna was both mother and teacher to her children, as they were forbidden to attend the Epworth school or even to play with the local children. She was a determined teacher.

Susanna began the education of each child when he or she reached the age of five, and on that first day the child was expected to learn the alphabet.[1] Well-educated herself and devoutly religious, Susanna taught the children Latin and Greek and the Bible, and examined them on their lessons twice a day. If a child failed in his or her lessons, behaved badly, or ate between meals, the child was beaten. After a beating, the child was "expected to cry softly."[2] When the sons of the family were old enough, they were expected to go to public school (the equivalent of private school in the United States); the daughters, however, were expected to marry.

John Wesley was sent to Charterhouse School in London at the age of ten and a half. Although the regime at such schools was strict, for young John Wesley it must have seemed idyllic after the isolation and discipline at home. As he had not yet started keeping his voluminous journal at that age, little is known of this time at Charterhouse except that he was not good at sports. His brother Samuel, thirteen years older than John, was also in London and was a scholar at Westminster School. He wrote to his father that "Jack is a brave boy, learning Hebrew as fast as he can."

John studied hard, and his achievements at Charterhouse, coupled with the excellent though arduous teachings of Susanna, enabled him to seek admission to Oxford University when sixteen years old. He was interviewed by Dr. Henry Sacheverell, a High Church Anglican and a Tory. "I found him alone," John wrote later, "as tall as a may-pole, and as fine as an archbishop. I was a very little fellow. . . . He said: 'You are too young to go to University; you cannot know Greek and Latin yet. Go back to school.' I looked at him as David looked at Goliath, and despised him in my heart. I thought: 'If I do not know Greek and Latin better than you, I ought to go back to school indeed.' I left him, and neither entreaties nor commands could have brought me back to him." Despite what John Wesley thought of Sacheverell, he held his tongue—as Susanna had taught him—and in 1720, just as he turned seventeen, became a member of Christ Church college at Oxford University, with a scholarship of £40 a year.

In Oxford, John Wesley found a place meant for just such as him. In many ways he felt he had, at last, found a home. Oxford provided both the spiritual and intellectual climate in which John could flourish. In 1725 he was ordained a deacon and preached his first sermon at South Leigh, near Witney. He was ordained a priest on September 22, 1728. John fully expected to spend the rest of his life at Oxford.

It has often been mistakenly assumed that John Wesley was, as he described himself, *homo unius libri*, a man of one book (the Bible). While the Bible was of utmost importance to him, he also drew from many other sources for his ideas. He read omnivorously; V. H. H. Green, in *The Young Mr. Wesley*, devotes fourteen pages alone to listing the books that Wesley read between 1725 and 1734, the years he spent at Oxford after being ordained. In 1726 he was elected to a fellowship at Lincoln College, the same year that Charles Wesley entered Oxford.[3]

The fellowship at Lincoln provided John with a room and modest salary of £28, to continue "so long as he remained celibate (which meant that he benefited from it till 1751)."[4] His duties included teaching Greek and philosophy, lecturing on passages from the Greek New Testament, and serving as moderator at the daily debates held at the university. The fellowship also allowed him to preach at various churches without the encumbrance of maintaining a parish and its daily business. Even at the start of his career, his vocation as an itinerant preacher seemed fated.

During this time also, John Wesley began organizing

his life in a systematic way that gave it more meaning for him. Susanna had organized the daily lessons of the children in the Epworth rectory so that no moment was wasted, and John took a leaf from her book, ordering his days "methodically." Mondays and Tuesdays were devoted to the study of Latin and Greek; on Wednesdays he studied logic and ethics; Thursdays, Hebrew and Arabic; Fridays, metaphysics and natural philosophy; Saturdays, rhetoric and poetics; and on Sunday, theology.

In addition to ordering his studies, he had earlier, in 1725, after reading Bishop Taylor's *Rules and Exercises of Holy Living and Dying*, drawn up "rules" for himself to follow in his daily life. Taylor's book was to shape John's entire life. It made him determined to dedicate all his thoughts, actions, and words to God. His rules seem aimed at that result:

A General Rule in All Actions of Life
Whenever you are to do an action, consider how God did or would do the like, and do you imitate his example.

General Rules of Employing Time
1. Begin and end every day with God; and sleep not immoderately.
2. Be diligent in your calling.
3. Employ all spare hours in religion; as able.
4. All hollidays [should be devoted to religion].
5. Avoid drunkards and busybodies.
6. Avoid curiosity, and all useless employments and knowledge.
7. Examine yourself every night.

8. Never on any account pass a day without setting aside at least an hour for devotion.
9. Avoid all manner of passion.

One might think from reading John Wesley's personal rules that here was a humorless, dour—and friendless—young man, but quite the opposite was true. While strict with himself, he did not impose his own discipline on others, and he was good-looking convivial company, admired for his intellect and wit. While a fellow at Lincoln College, one of John's closest friends was Robert Kirkham of Merton College. He invited John—"the little and handsome person," as he described him—to visit at his home. Kirkham was the son of the vicar of the village of Stanton in the Cotswolds, and in his home John was to find lively and amiable companionship in Robert, his sisters Sally and Betty, and their neighbors, Ann and Mary Granville.

Each of the young people adopted a nickname. John (known as "Cyrus") was especially taken with the pretty and intelligent "Varanese" (Sally Kirkham). For some time it seemed that she was also taken with him. He was handsome and could dance, sing, ride, swim, and conduct challenging conversations in the group. At one point John questioned in his diary, "Meeting with a religious friend, which I never till now had, I began to alter the whole form of my conversation. . . . Have I loved woman or company more than God?"

Later, Sally was to write to him, "When I first saw you the utmost I desired was to take my hand round your neck. . . . I was afraid then; it was only the improbability of attaining them that made me so moderate in my wishes." Whether frightened by young Wesley's intensity or his intellect, Sally chose to marry another clergyman, Jack Chapone.

John Wesley took Sally's marriage with good grace, attending her wedding and remaining her friend all his life. The expectations he might have had, however, are revealed in a letter from his sister, Emilia, in whom he had confided. She wrote,

> Had you not lost your dear Mrs. C———n, where had your love been fixed? On heaven, I hope, principally; but a large share, too, had been hers: you would not have been so spiritualized, but something of this lower world would have had its part in your heart, wise as you are; but being deprived of her there went all hope of worldly happiness: and now the mind, which is an active principle, losing its aim here, has fixed on its Maker for happiness.

John should find consolation in the spiritual, Emilia advised, from losses here in this world. Sally would only have deprived him of a measure of his spirituality if he had married her.

Whether because of the loss of Sally Kirkham or from a true sense of devotion, in 1727 John returned home to Epworth to help his father. Samuel, who at the time was working on a massive book on Job, in addition to carrying out his parish duties, had had a stroke. While those in Epworth were no longer hostile to him, he was having difficulty also ministering to those in his cure of Wroote. He needed a curate to take over his duties there and he called upon John.

John returned home to help temporarily, feeling that he could continue his studies there just as easily as at Oxford. Little of the preaching ability he was to show later in life was exhibited in Wroote, however. As he himself noted later in his journal, "From the year 1725 to 1729 I preached much, but saw no fruit of my labour."

The Wesley household in Epworth was still beset by debt and Samuel's obduracy. During this time, John's sister Hetty fell in love and ran off with a local lawyer, only to part from him after twenty-four hours. When she returned home, she found that Samuel had ordered that her name was never to be mentioned in the house. After pleading with him, she was accepted back, but only on the condition that she marry the first suitor to propose. This turned out to be William Wright, a plumber, who moved with Hetty to London. William soon took to drink, and Hetty and her children slowly perished, not only from neglect but also from lead poisoning, caused by lead water pipes in the poor sections of London (the wealthier areas had copper pipes). Although her brothers tried to help her, there was little they could do. In Samuel's eyes, she was doing penance for her wickedness.

In 1729 the rector of Lincoln College, Dr. Morley, wrote to John Wesley, reminding him that, as a moderator of the college, John was required to live there if he wished to keep his fellowship. "Your father may certainly have another curate," Dr. Morley wrote, "though not so much to his satisfaction." Samuel was not pleased; he had hoped that John would continue ministering to Wroote and, when Samuel retired or died, take over Epworth. John, however, assured a modest living in Oxford without the privations and debt of Epworth, was quite willing to return to Lincoln College.

While John Wesley had been at Oxford, in addition to

his study of philosophy and languages, he had been exploring the idea of a life of spirituality in his readings. Initially he had been "influenced by the Cambridge Platonists, Smith and Cudworth, who pointed to an experience of interiority whereby the inward world of spirituality rather than the outward world became one's authentic habitat."[5] In 1725, however, as was mentioned, he read *Rules and Exercises of Holy Living and Dying*. This came to overshadow much of his other reading and led to his "methodizing" his life. But John was still not satisfied. He felt, after reading William Law's *Christian Perfection* and *Serious Call*, that he was not doing enough. Law wrote of the impossibility of being "half a Christian;" one must devote oneself entirely to God. John felt he had failed in doing this. "Christian perfection, perfect love, became and remained Wesley's purpose in following the Christian way."[6] As Wesley was later to write in *A Plain Account of Genuine Christianity* (1753), a person, in order to be a full Christian, "willingly resigns all he is, all he has, to His [God's] wise and gracious disposal. The ruling temper of his heart is the most absolute submission and the tenderest gratitude to his sovereign benefactor."

In 1729, John Wesley was just starting the journey that would culminate in these ideas. In 1729 he felt that he lacked the true spirituality of a Christian and was casting about for the means to achieve it.

John Wesley's return to Oxford marked the beginning of his quest for spirituality, a search that would eventually result in a set of ideas that would become known as Methodism. Ironically, it was his younger brother, Charles, who had always followed in John's footsteps, who would start him on his way.

IV

The Holy Club

THE YOUNGEST AND LAST SON OF SAMUEL WESLEY, Charles dwelt in the shadows of his two older brothers, Samuel and John. His older brother Samuel was a distant voice. Seventeen years separated the two, and Charles viewed him more as a father-figure, particularly while at school.

At the age of nine, Charles had been sent to Westminster School in London, which Samuel also attended. Samuel looked after Charles who eventually became a King's Scholar and captain of the school. Like his father, Samuel had a talent for poetry and frequented the company of Alexander Pope, Matthew Prior, and Jonathan Swift. Because of Samuel's interests, Charles too tried his hand at poetry—with good

results—and benefited from the literary influence of his
elder brother and his friends.

With a richer literary and more worldly background
than John, Charles started college in 1727 at Christ
Church, Oxford University. Later he described himself
at this time as preoccupied with "harmless diversions"
that kept him "dead to God, and asleep in the arms of
Satan for eighteen years." Although he was being a bit
hard on himself, his brother John commented, "He pur-
sued his studies diligently and led a regular harmless
life: but if I spoke to him about religion he would
warmly answer: 'What, would you have me be a saint
all at once?'" More than John Wesley, Charles was tast-
ing life, although the stringent upbringing in Epworth
and his lack of money kept him from straying too far.

During the time John Wesley was at Wroote, however,
Charles suddenly had a change of heart regarding religion. What triggered it is unknown—even to Charles,
as he wrote to John: "It is owing in great measure to
somebody's prayers (my mother's, most likely) that I am
come to think as I do; for I cannot tell myself how or
when I first woke out of my lethargy, only that it was
not long after you went away." Rather prophetically,
Charles sought spiritual help from John, saying, "There
is no one person I would so willingly have to be the
instrument of good to me as you. It is through your
means, I firmly believe, that God will accomplish what
He hath begun in me."

Like John, Charles sought to "order" his life, and to
this purpose formed a group composed initially of himself, Robert Kirkham, and an Irish youth, William Morgan. The young men met to study and to seek a

Christian way of life, drawn together by a common interest and a desire for discussion.

When John Wesley returned from Wroote, Charles immediately introduced him into the group and, with his organizational talents and drive for order, John assumed leadership, to unanimous approval. Taking his personal rules as a model, he proposed a system of daily self-examination for the members of the group. It included asking oneself questions such as:

1. Have I been simple and recollected in everything I said or did?
2. Have I prayed with fervor? at going in and out of church? in the church? morning and evening in private?
3. Have I duly used ejaculations? that is, have I every hour prayed for humility, faith, hope, love, and the particular virtue of the day?

As the little group grew, it began meeting each day from six until nine to pray, recite psalms, study the Greek New Testament, and speak of their own and others' shortcomings. Every Sunday they took Communion, although the Anglican Church required it only three times a year. The members were enjoined to pray for a few minutes every hour each day, and to fast on Wednesdays and Fridays.

John led with an easy hand. As one member, John Gambold, later wrote of the meetings,

> Mr. John Wesley was always the chief manager, for which he was very fit. . . . Yet he never assumed anything to himself above his companions. Any of them

might speak their mind, and their words were as strictly regarded by him as his were by them.

The group began to be noticed by others at Oxford, not always favorably. As John wrote,

> A gentleman of Merton College, who was one of our little company, which now consisted of five persons, acquainted us that he had been much rallied the day before for being a member of *The Holy Club;* . . . some men of wit in Christ Church . . . made a pretty many reflections upon the *Sacramentarians,* as they were pleased to call us. . . . It was soon reported that Dr. ——— — and the censors were going to blow up *The Godly Club.* . . . We were sometimes dignified with [the name] of *The Enthusiasts,* or *The Reforming Club.* . . . As for the names of *Methodists, Supererogationmen* and so on. . . .

Like so many groups which strike out on their own, the young men drew to themselves various derogatory names. However, they turned the derogatory into something of which they were proud, calling themselves "The Holy Club." It is also in this connection that the appellation "Methodist" was first applied to the ideas of John and Charles Wesley.

Although he was devotedly following the strict regime of the Holy Club, John still felt that he had failed in some way—he was not doing enough. He strove to "keep His [God's] *whole law,* inward and outward, *to the utmost of my power.* . . ." One means was delivered to him in 1730, when William Morgan revealed that he had been visiting the prisons to spread Christianity and

education. The club's members seized upon the idea
enthusiastically. As John wrote in his journal in 1738:

> In 1730 I began visiting the prisons, assisting the poor
> and sick in town, and doing what other good I could by
> my presence or my little fortune to the bodies and souls
> of all men. To this end I abridged myself of all super-
> fluities, and many that are called necessaries of life. I
> soon became a *by-word* for so doing. . . . I omitted no
> occasion of doing good. I for that reason suffered
> evil. . . .

The actions of the members of the Holy Club were
derided by their fellow students and dimly viewed by
the university authorities. John and Charles Wesley
were beginning to encounter the opposition to their
ideas that would plague them all their lives as Methodists. One young man, Richard Morgan, wrote home
scornfully from Oxford that,

> There is a Society of gentlemen consisting of seven
> members, whom the world calls Methodists, of whom
> my tutor is President. They imagine they cannot be
> saved if they do not spend every hour, nay, every minute
> of their lives in the service of God. To that end they read
> prayers every day in the common jail . . . they endeavor
> to reform notorious whores. . . . They rise every day at
> five of the clock. A religious book is read all the time we
> are together. Though some are remarkable for eating
> very heartily on gaudy-days, they stint themselves by
> two pence meat, and a farthing bread, and a draught of
> water when they dine at their own expense . . .

Richard Morgan, as John Wesley's student, was lumped

in with the members of the Holy Club in the eyes of the other students and called by "the name of a Methodist, the misfortune of which I cannot describe."

John Wesley, unfortunately, saw a copy of Morgan's letter and castigated him in a letter of his own to Morgan's father, at the same time demonstrating the intentional exclusivity of the Holy Club:

> Of his [Richard Morgan's] being admitted into our Society . . . there is no danger. All these gentlemen . . . would oppose me to the utmost should I attempt to introduce among them, at those important hours, one of whose prudence I had so short a trial and who was so little experienced in piety and charity.

Although part of an exclusive group at Oxford, most of the members of the Holy Club would go on to lead ordinary lives. As the club members grew older, the cares of the world began to intrude upon their isolation. Not only did the members feel obliged to do charitable works nearby, but they began to feel that they should go farther afield. One idea in particular seemed to strike John Wesley's fancy, spurred by the return of General James Edward Oglethorpe (1696–1785) from the New World where he had established a British settlement at what is now Savannah, Georgia.

On Oglethorpe's return voyage he had brought with him six Creek Indians, including their chief, Tomo-Chi-Chi. Tomo-Chi-Chi was the wonder of London. He was entertained by the king, the archbishop of Canterbury and the masters and students of Eton College. Crowds flocked to see him, among them John Wesley and his sister Kezia. Returning to Oxford with tales of the colonization of Georgia and of its "noble savages," John and the other members of the Holy Club debated the idea of traveling to America. John, Charles, and Benjamin Ingham of the club, along with another acquaintance, Charles Delamotte, who "had offered himself some days before," decided to travel to Georgia with Oglethorpe's next expedition to missionize the Indians and the Georgian colonists.

John quickly wrote to Dr. John Burton, whose task it was to choose the clergyman who would accompany Oglethorpe. "My chief motive," John wrote, "is the hope of saving my own soul. I hope to learn the true sense of the gospel of Christ by preaching it to the heathen. They have no comments to construe away the text. . . . By these, therefore, I hope to learn the purity of that faith which was once delivered to the saints."

Although John's stated motive was to increase his spirituality, a more mundane one may have influenced his decision. Samuel had written John a few months previously that he hoped John would return to assume the duties of the Epworth parish. Then over seventy, Samuel was no longer able to keep up with his tasks as rector. John had written back at length, declining Samuel's appeal, but his reasons may have seemed weak even to himself. "Freedom from care," he wrote, "I take to be the next greatest advantage to freedom from useless and therefore hurtful company. And this too I enjoy in greater perfection here [at Oxford] than I can ever expect to do anywhere else." Going off to do God's work—to missionize among the heathen—might have seemed a nobler excuse to John Wesley than that he was comfortable at Oxford. Whatever the reason, Dr. Burton accepted the offer of the members of the Holy Club, only insisting that Charles Wesley be ordained before leaving.

Charles was reluctant to go to Georgia but, as usual, John's plans came first. Charles was later to write, "I took my degree and only thought of spending all my days at Oxford. But my brother, who always had the ascendant over me, persuaded me to accompany him and Mr. Oglethorpe to Georgia. I exceedingly dreaded entering into Holy Orders but he over-ruled me here also, and I was ordained deacon by the Bishop of Oxford, and the next Sunday, priest by the Bishop of London."

On October 14, 1735, John and Charles Wesley, Benjamin Ingham, and Charles Delamotte set sail for America aboard the *Simmonds*. Charles would be serving as secretary to the new colony's governor, General Oglethorpe, and John would be Savannah's rector. For both, the voyage would prove an enlightening experience indeed, and, for John Wesley, a significant step on the road to Methodism.

V

A Journey Toward Faith

JOHN WESLEY'S JOURNEY TO THE NEW WORLD WAS BOTH A physical and a spiritual one. At Oxford he had reached a sort of spiritual impasse, questioning the strength of his own faith and the value of going out to help others. As he reflected in his journal in 1738:

> . . . a contemplative man convinced me still more than I was convinced before that outward works are nothing, being alone; and in several conversations instructed me how to pursue inward holiness, or a union of the soul with God.

Wesley, however, had become convinced that the way

45

he was praying—"mental prayer"—was just as ego-
tistical as the doing of good works. The "union of the
soul with God" was proving more elusive to him than
ever.

On board the *Simmonds* this was again brought
home to John in his encounter with a group of twenty-
six Moravians, German missionaries from Count
Zinzendorf's sanctuary of Herrnhut. He wrote in his
journal that he "had long observed the great se-
riousness of their behavior. Of their humility they had
given a continual proof, by performing those servile
offices for the other passengers, which none of the
English would undertake; for which they desired, and
would receive no pay, saying, 'it was good for their
proud hearts', and 'their loving Savior had done more
for them.'"

The young men from Oxford had continued the regime of the Holy Club even on board ship, but John saw,
in the simple tasks performed by the Moravians, a
humility and piety that he felt he was lacking. This
seemed to be confirmed when the ship encountered a
fierce storm that threatened the lives of all on board:

> . . . the sea broke over, split the mainsail in pieces,
> covered the ship, and poured in between the decks, as if
> the great deep had already swallowed us up. A terrible
> screaming began among the English. The Germans
> calmly sung on. I asked one of them afterwards, "Was
> you not afraid?" He answered. "I thank God, no." I
> asked, "But were not your women and children afraid?"
> He replied mildly, "No; our women and children are
> not afraid to die."
>
> From them I went to their crying, trembling neigh-
> bors, and pointed out to them the difference in the hour

of trial, between him that feareth God, and him that
feareth Him not.

Young John Wesley marveled at the depth of the
Moravians' faith. In his discussions with them, he tried
to learn from them but, as he commented in 1738, "I
understood it not at first. I was too learned and too
wise, so that it seemed foolishness unto me. And I
continued preaching and following after, and trusting
in that righteousness whereby no flesh can be justified." John Wesley was troubled more than spiritually
on the trip, however. In his naiveté and zeal he alienated a great many of the company, and two ladies in
particular, which was to prove disastrous later, in Savannah.

In an effort to carry on as they had at Oxford, the
Holy Club members held frequent services and readings and insisted on prayers twice a day. "The people,"
John wrote, "were angry at my expounding so often."
Two ladies, however, welcomed the good-looking
young minister's attentions: Mrs. Hawkins, whose hus-
band was the settlement's new doctor; and Mrs. Welsh,
who was expecting a child. General Oglethorpe had
given his cabin to Mrs. Welsh because of her condition
and John Wesley visited the two women there each day.
But while he was intent upon the spiritual side of life,
the ladies were taken with this intense, handsome
young man and flirted with him unabashedly. When it
became evident that their coquettishness was having
no effect, they became openly hostile: "Hell hath no
fury like a woman scorned."

John further alienated the colonists once they arrived
in Savannah. General Oglethorpe had decreed that both

rum and slavery were forbidden in the new colony and John righteously took it upon himself to carry out the governor's orders, staving in several cases of rum.

In Savannah John Wesley had little opportunity to save his own soul or "learn the true sense of the gospel of Christ by preaching it to the heathen." His parish duties kept him fully occupied, duties he was not quite prepared to handle. Not even his experiences on board ship had taught him that all were not as devoted to God as he.

John's parish included nearly 700 people and he set out to order it as methodically as he had the Holy Club. On Sundays he held three services and a children's class, with prayers in French and Italian in between. "I began," he wrote, "visiting my parishioners in order, from house to house; for which I set apart . . . viz. from twelve till three in the afternoon [each day]." John also rigidly enforced attendance at Sunday services and adopted the practice of baptism by immersion from the Primitive Church. When one woman refused to have her child "dipped," he denied it baptism.

Mrs. Hawkins' tongue had not stopped wagging against the new settlement's minister when they arrived and, unfortunately, the stringency of John's rules gave her even more to discuss. His insistence on Sunday observances led John to have Dr. Hawkins confined to the guardroom for hunting on the Sabbath. One of the doctor's patients had a miscarriage while he was being so held, and indignation against Mr. Wesley swept the settlement.

The hostility was exacerbated when John received a letter from Charles, in Frederica, which referred to Mrs. Hawkins and Mrs. Welsh. Somehow Mrs. Hawkins found out about it and, inviting John to her home, threatened to shoot him. He escaped with only a torn sleeve after her terrified servants summoned the constable.

Mrs. Hawkins was not finished with the Wesleys, however. She and Mrs. Welsh set out to ruin Charles in the eyes of General Oglethorpe, whom he served as secretary. Mrs. Hawkins approached Oglethorpe with the information that Charles and Mrs. Welsh were having an adulterous affair. Oglethorpe had him watched and found that Charles did indeed visit Mrs. Welsh, for she had invited him to her home on the pretext of spiritual counseling. Suspected and harassed, Charles fell ill with dysentery and appealed to his brother John for help. When John arrived and heard of the situation, he was incensed. He went to Oglethorpe and cleared the matter up, as well as straightening out the general's papers, which Charles had let fall into disarray. Oglethorpe, however, felt that the whole incident had hurt the colony, and that for Charles to remain would merely keep tongues wagging. Charles was sent back to England, supposedly as a courier for Oglethorpe, and never returned.

John went back to his own hornet's nest of problems in Savannah. As he wrote in his journal at that time, "I knew that *the law* of God was *spiritual; I consented to it that it was good. Yea, I delighted in it after the inner man. Yet was I carnel, sold under sin.*" The incident to which he is referring was probably his dalliance with Miss Sophy Hopkey, the niece of the chief magistrate of Savannah.

Sophy, a pretty girl with a number of suitors, began to pay special attention to John Wesley. One might assume that John would have learned some kind of lesson from the machinations of Mrs. Hawkins, but in his dealings with Sophy he displayed the same naiveté as before. Initially Sophy dropped by the parsonage for prayers, but soon she was also taking French lessons from John and consulting with him on gardening, a special interest of his.

John had earlier noticed Sophy on the voyage to Georgia but surrendered completely during an illness through which she nursed him (John Wesley was to show a particular weakness for women who nursed him in illness). Despite Sophy's expectations after John had recovered, he was not able to abandon himself to her charms. Leaving the settlement on the pretext of business, he sent a note to Sophy:

> I find, Miss Sophy, that I can't take fire into my bosom, and not be burnt. I am therefore retiring for a while to desire the direction of God. Join with me, my friend, in fervent prayer that He would show me what is best to be done.

On his return, he told Sophy that he had come to the decision not to marry "till I have been among the Indians," still feeling that only among the heathen could he find the spiritual happiness which he sought.

Sophy was hardly happy with this resolution. Soon John received a letter from her aunt announcing her forthcoming wedding to a Mr. Williamson and asking John to publish the banns. Feeling that the couple did not fulfill the High Church standards he had established, John refused to marry them, much to their displeasure. Sophy and William Williamson were married in the Carolina colony, where moral standards were less strict.

The matter might have died down, and life become peaceful for John in Savannah, but he continued to occupy himself with Sophy. He felt that she was falling away from the church. On August 7, 1737, as he wrote, "I repelled Mrs. Williamson from the Holy Communion, for the reasons specified in my letter of July 5, as well as for not giving me notice of her design to communicate after having intermitted it for some time." For a small community like Savannah, such an event was a scandal.

The next day Sophy's uncle had John arrested for defamation of her character. John appeared in court and was arraigned and released without bail on his own word. His trial, during the next court session, began with a long list of complaints against him, on some of which he was found guilty. Now all the animosity that he had engendered for himself on board ship and in Savannah returned to haunt him. Although forbidden to leave Savannah, such opposition forced John to flee, making his tortuous way overland to Charleston, South Carolina, where he found a boat bound for England. On Christmas Eve of 1737 he sailed from America. He had come with "the hope of saving my own soul," but left to save his life.

Young John Wesley blamed, not the people of Savannah, but himself. If only he had a "sure trust and confidence in God"—the spiritual faith that he had so desperately sought all his life—he would not have failed. Just as he had suffered a spiritual crisis on leaving England, he suffered again on his return. Yet this time an answer was at hand.

In my return to England, January 1738, being in immi-
nent danger of death and very uneasy on that account, I
was strongly convinced that the cause of that un-
easiness was unbelief and that the gaining of a true,
living faith was the one thing needful for me. But still I
fixed not this faith on its right object: I meant only faith
in God, not faith in or through Christ. . . . So that when
Peter Böhler, whom God prepared for me as soon as I
came to London, affirmed of true faith in Christ (which
is but one) that it had those two fruits inseparably
attending it, "dominion over sin, and constant peace
from a sense of forgiveness." I was quite amazed and
looked upon it as a new Gospel. If this was so, it was
clear I had not faith. But I was not willing to be convinced of this.

Peter Böhler was a Moravian pastor in London. The
Moravian Brethren were Pietist in orientation, believ-
ing that Christ was a "gracious friend" who "died here
for my sake," and that "Christ dwells in the believer
and brings him to a life of holiness."[1] This transforma-
tion to a holy way of life was not instantaneous but
rather gradual. Count Zinzendorf of Saxony had ex-
pounded on this view and encouraged the sect, saying,
"We cannot know God in himself, but only through the
Son, and the Son we know essentially by feeling," and
"perfect love casts out fear."[2]

Böhler diagnosed John's trouble as a "lack of Saving
Faith." John asked Böhler if that meant that he should
abandon preaching. Böhler answered: " 'By no means.'
I asked, 'But what shall I preach?' He said, 'Preach faith
till you have it; and then, because you have it, you will
preach faith!' Accordingly . . . I began preaching this

new doctrine, though my soul started back from the work."[3]

In opposition to the Calvinistic predestination encompassed in Anglican doctrine, John Wesley began to emphasize justification by faith alone in his sermons, a significant step for one who had staunchly adhered to the teachings of the Church of England. The seeds of a new way of thinking—and a new denomination—were being sown.

Ever the organizer, in May of 1738 John formed a religious group in Fetter Lane in London. The members met on Wednesdays to pray together and exhort each other; every fourth Sunday was to be a day of intercession; and every fifth Sunday a general "love-feast." A love feast had two features: a distribution of bread and water; and spiritual testimony. The distribution of bread and water was not Communion, however; that was the sole province of the church. It was comparable to a fellowship meal and not intended to replace the Lord's Supper. At this time John Wesley had no thought or desire to break away from the Church of England. He had been strictly reared in the church; his father, Samuel, had denounced dissenters vehemently and had taken an Anglican line in all matters. It did not occur to John to question the basic authority of the church. Yet, little by little—so gradually that he did not notice—he was moving away from it and toward a spiritual and, later a physical "conversion."

VI

"Where Is Thy Joy?"

ALTHOUGH JOHN WESLEY ASSIDUOUSLY SET OUT TO DO AS Peter Böhler said—to preach the faith—it was not until May of 1738 that he felt the touch of that faith. Many Methodists today date the true start of Methodism from that moment, although it would be several years (not until 1744, in fact) before any sort of formal organization appeared.

On May 24, 1738, John Wesley rose early and, as was his custom, opened his Bible at random. The passages before him seemed propitious and,

In the evening I went very unwillingly to a society in Aldersgate Street, where one was reading Luther's preface to the Epistle to the Romans. About a quarter before nine, while he was describing the change which God works in the heart through faith in Christ, I felt my heart strangely warmed. I felt I did trust in Christ, Christ alone for salvation; and an assurance was given me that He had taken away *my* sins, even *mine*, and saved *me* from the law of sin and death.

I began to pray with all my might for those who had in a more especial manner despitefully used me and persecuted me. I then testified openly to all there what I now first felt in my heart. But it was not long before the enemy suggested, "This cannot be faith; for where is thy joy?" Then was I taught that peace and victory over sin are essential to faith in the Captain of our salvation; but that, as to the transports of joy that usually attend the beginning of it, especially in those who have mourned deeply, God sometimes giveth, sometimes withholdeth them, according to the counsels of His own will.

At last, he felt, he knew the serenity which the Moravians had demonstrated on the ship bound for America and, later, in their group in London. This idea of personal salvation through the grace of God was to become a keystone of Wesley's movement. Later, in a sermon entitled "Working Out Your Own Salvation," he explained that "even in a state of sin every man possesses some spark of original grace, sufficient to enable him to turn. It is by the grace of God that he turns, but *he* turns."[1] This doctrine of grace is central to Wesley's theology.

Charles shared in the exhilaration which John experienced at Aldersgate, having three days before, reportedly, undergone a similar revelation. Both brothers joined together to spread the word of their experiences.

John, however, initially was so moved that he alarmed friends and family alike, prompting his older brother Samuel to write, "I heartily pray God to stop the progress of this lunacy."

Because of the Moravians' influence upon him, John traveled to Germany to see their colony at Herrnhut. Although he felt it was "a happy place," after his visit he began to have doubts about their way of worship. They were *too* complacent, he felt, neglected the means of grace (ritual), and ignored what he believed was an obligation to do good works; they isolated themselves from their fellow men rather than going among them to preach salvation. John still felt that a *method* to salvation, through a combination of theology, ritual and action, was needed.

On his return to England, John read accounts of the impressive results that Jonathan Edwards had achieved by preaching to crowds in New England in 1737. Although he did not agree with Edwards' Calvinistic theology, John could not ignore the effectiveness of his *method*. So, on March 29, 1739, when he was asked by George Whitefield to take over his preaching in Bristol while he himself traveled to America, John could not refuse the opportunity to try his hand at Edwards' approach.

Whitefield had been a late arrival to the Holy Club at Oxford, only being introduced as a member in 1735, after coming to the aid of an old woman in a workhouse who had tried to cut her throat. Like Wesley, he was later inspired by accounts of the preaching of the American Jonathan Edwards. While Wesley would see Edwards' techniques as proof of the need to go among the people to preach and educate, Whitefield would see in them not only a reinforcement of his own Calvinistic doctrine, but also evidence of the success of dramatic presentation in spreading the word. Whitefield developed an effective preaching style, but it was so theatrical that his Anglican superiors eventually removed him from the pulpit for his "ranting and raving."

In America, Whitefield took to open air preaching, as would become characteristic among revivalists. His style of preaching got results. After one of his sermons during his tour in America, according to a contemporary account, "some were struck pale as Death, others wringing their hands, others lying on the ground, others sinking into the arms of their friends, and most lifting up their eyes toward heaven, and crying out to GOD." His dramatic oratory drew crowds of thousands. In Philadelphia alone, Whitefield spoke from the gallery of the courthouse to a crowd of 6,000 people standing in the streets below.

Back in England, John Wesley was also finding success with Whitefield's approach. On April 2, 1739, he noted, "I submitted to be more vile, and proclaimed in the highways the glad tidings of salvation, speaking from a little emminence in a ground adjoining to the city, to about three thousand people." It was the first time that John had preached to so great a crowd outside a church. The results were beyond his expectations; people were moved to frenzies of joy and repentance.

Whitefield had called upon John Wesley not only to fill in for him, but also to organize—to "methodize"— the crowds who were drawn to him. As he had in London, John immediately began forming societies to bring order to the movement and also began expanding its size and its horizons. In so doing, John stressed the idea of "connection." The various groups were connected one to another by itinerant ministers and also, in John's mind, connected to the Church of England. Even after ties with the church were severed, this idea of connection prevailed, the Methodists often being referred to as the "Methodist Connection."

The large, outdoor gatherings and small, fervent groups hardly went unnoticed by the Church of England or the general public. Disapproval was widespread, not only of these new Methodists, but of all dissenting groups who, taking a page from Edwards' and Whitefield's book, demonstrated the "enthusiasm" of the new revivalism. The great satirical cartoonist Hogarth portrayed the "credulity, superstition and fanaticism" of these new Methodists who physically and spiritually threw themselves into their religion. Members of the established church attacked the two Wesley brothers orally and in print. One, a Dr. Trapp, warned, "Go not after the impostors and seducers; but shun them as you would the plague." As John and Charles traveled about, they were threatened with violence more than once; fortunately, they were usually able to avoid harm.

The idea of spreading salvation and education among the masses threatened both the British class system and the prevailing mores. "The insurgency of Methodism was a sign of something profoundly evolving in the temper of the time, the passing of the phase of reason and judgement in favour of that of passion and 'possession.' "[2] And with their traditional reserve, the sedate British were shocked by the manifestations of frenzy and the physical convulsions experienced by some of those who were "taken" by this new religious movement.

From the quiet of his own reserve and the orderliness of his "method," even John Wesley was at times alarmed. At Wapping, for example, after his sermon, "many of those that heard began to call upon God with strong cries and tears. Some sank down, and there remained no strength in them; others exceedingly trembled and quaked; some were torn with a kind of convulsive motion. . . . I have seen many hysterical and many epileptic fits; but none of them were like these." As Methodism took hold, however, these frenzied responses died down, much to Wesley's relief.

With the beginnings of organization among the new Methodists came conflicts with old friends. In 1740 John Wesley broke away from the Moravians and was moving away from George Whitefield. The Moravians disapproved of actively seeking salvation through deeds and of the hoopla of Wesley's huge, outdoor meetings. In July, John was told that he could no longer preach in the Moravian meeting place on Fetter Lane. Stung, but convinced that he was right in all that he was doing, John wrote to them with his own complaints, ending, "But as I find you more and more confirmed in the error of your ways, nothing new remains but that I should give you up to God. You that are of the same judgement, follow me."

John's dispute with Whitefield stemmed from Whitefield's strong Calvinist belief in predestination. "No scripture can mean that God is not love," Wesley had emphasized. This was in direct conflict with Whitefield's more traditional "hellfire and damnation" views.

Although the two men continued cordial relations, the close ties that had bound them in the Holy Club were severed.

That same year, John decided that the movement needed a base of operations in London from which preachers and lay-preachers could be sent out to organize. Although strapped financially—his only steady income continued to be the £28 a year from his Oxford fellowship—John managed to raise nearly £1,000 to lease and refurbish an abandoned foundry near Moorfield. Remodeled, with a school and a meeting room that could hold 300 people, it also included living quarters for John and for his mother, Susanna, because Samuel Wesley had died. The foundry served as headquarters for the Methodist movement until 1778, when the City Road Chapel was opened.[3] Methodism was now firmly entrenched in England, with a headquarters and the beginnings of an organization that would eventually reach around the world.

While John Wesley was laying down both the physical and theological foundations of Methodism, his brother Charles was not idle. After his own conversion experience of May 21, 1738, Charles felt he had to put that experience into a form which everyone could share. He turned to one familiar to him, the hymn. Always comfortable with writing poetry as a boy, and having written or adapted hymns while in Georgia, Charles now found his true "voice" and vocation. Like John he traveled and preached, but he is most remembered for the hymns that he composed throughout his life for the use of the Methodists. Characterized by great feeling, his hymns have moved Methodists and non-Methodists alike. Such emotion is seen in the first hymn that he wrote after his conversion, which embodies the sense of celebration which filled his heart at the idea that salvation was available to all:

> Outcasts of men, to you I call,
> Harlots and publicans, and thieves!
> He spreads his arms to embrace you all:
> Sinners alone his grace receive;
> No need of him the righteous have;
> He came the lost to seek and save.

Although rough, this hymn conveys the idea of going out to bring the word of God to all walks of life. At last, this hymn proclaimed, here was a sect that, rather than damning them for their poverty and sins, as did the Calvinists, went to the sinners and told them that they could rise above their condition.

Following the lead of his brother John, who had previously published a number of volumes of hymns, in 1745 Charles published his own *Hymns on the Lord's Supper*, for use by the Methodists. This was to be but the first in a series of collections of his hymns, some of which have influenced and moved the world. Few non-Methodists are aware of the fact that both "Hark, the Herald-Angels Sing" and "Christ the Lord Is Risen Today" were penned by the quiet young Methodist minister who was so often overshadowed by his more famous brother.

With such moving hymns and John's prowess as a preacher and organizer, it is no wonder that Methodism soon spread throughout England. Yet it was still connected to the Church of England. John's stated aim was "not to form any new sect; but to reform the nation, particularly the Church; and to spread Scriptural holiness over the land."

In order to be more effective, John had organized his group into societies, classes, bands, and select societies, and the conference was meant to be the ruling body. In 1744, John organized his first conference, consisting of six Anglican ministers and four lay preachers, at the foundry just outside London. The discussion turned to theological matters. As he wrote in *A Plain Account of Christian Perfection*, "The next morning after the conference began we seriously considered the doctrine of sanctification, or perfection. The questions asked concerning it and the substance of the answers given were as follows:

Q. What is it to be *sanctified?*
A. To be renewed in the image of God, *in righteousness and true holiness.*
Q. What is implied in being *a perfect Christian?*
A. The loving of God with all our heart, and mind, and soul (Deut. 6:5).
Q. Does this imply that *all inward sin* is taken away?
A. Undoubtedly: or how can we be said to be *saved from all our uncleanness* (Ezek. 36:29)."

To many the Conference of 1744 marks the beginning of Methodism, for it put into place and formalized the organizational structure, although the movement's ties with the Church of England were still as strong as ever. From their base in London, John and Charles traveled extensively in all weather. They were supplemented in their work by a number of like-minded Anglican clergy and a large number of lay preachers; as Methodism was

not a denomination, John did not feel that he could
ordain preachers. The "joy" John had felt briefly at his
own conversion was, thanks to them, spreading
through the towns and villages of England—and even
beyond its shores, to the new land of America.

VII

"The Best of All Is—God Is With Us!"

IN 1748 JOHN WESLEY HAD ANOTHER CLOSE BRUSH WITH romance, again with a woman who nursed him in illness. Grace Murray was a widow who had been converted to Methodism early and who had proven herself a dependable worker for the movement. In Newcastle she had been placed in charge of the orphans' home which the Methodists had built. Because of her abilities, John had chosen her to be among the group that traveled with him from town to town as he preached;

her job on these trips was to conduct classes for the women and girls.

When John fell ill in Newcastle, Grace quite naturally nursed him, as she had others in their entourage previously. As with Sophy Hopkey, John fell in love with his ministering angel. However, his practical instincts extended even into the area of romance, as is seen by his musings in his diary:

> I now clearly perceive, that my Marriage would bring little Expense if I married one I maintain now, who would afterwards desire nothing more than she had before. And would cheerfully consent, that our children (if any) should be wholly brought up at Kingswood. . . . I am persuaded she is in every Capacity an Help meet for me.

After his recovery, John made a rather circumspect proposal to Grace Murray and, with the understanding that they would be married sometime, started on another preaching tour, taking Grace in the accompanying group. In Yorkshire, John left Grace at the home of John Bennet, another preacher. She was to help Bennet on a preaching tour of his own.

Unbeknownst to John Wesley, Bennet had been in love with Grace for some time. Earlier he had proposed to her and, during their tour, he renewed his advances. Pressured, Grace finally told him that she would consent, if John Wesley agreed. Both sent letters to Wesley. The letters somehow gave him the impression that they were already married and he replied with good grace, accepting the situation. What then ensued was a confusion almost equal to his romantic troubles in Georgia.

Although betrothed to Bennet, Grace traveled with John Wesley to Wales where he officiated at Charles' marriage to Sarah Gwynne on April 3, 1749. Afterward, John and Grace traveled on to Ireland to preach. During their travels, their attraction to one another revived and, once again at Newcastle, they determined to marry. Charles, upon hearing of this, was extremely upset and rode post haste to stop the marriage. As John later wrote, "The thought of my marrying at all, but especially of my marrying a Servant, and one so low-born, appear'd above measure shocking to him. Thence he infer'd that it would break up all our Societies, and put a stop to the whole work of God."

When Charles arrived in Newcastle, John was at Whitehaven preaching. Charles confronted Grace and berated her, saying she was to marry Bennet. With Grace behind him, Charles rode to Bennet's home where the two were married a few days after. John Wesley, in his writings, seems not to blame Charles for his impetuous action; his tone is more that of resigned sorrow: "If I had had more Regard for her I loved than for the Work of God, I should now have gone straight on to Newcastle, and not back to Whitehaven." Once again John's vacillation had cost him a woman who might have made a good wife. He was, at forty-five, convinced that he should marry; his eventual choice, however, proved disastrous.

In 1751, John Wesley once again fell prey to the charms of a ministering angel. On February 10, having suffered a fall from his horse on London Bridge, he was carried to the home of a Mrs. Mary Vazeille, a wealthy Methodist widow. Mrs. Vazeille had several children and was known for her charm and grace, both of which she must have lavished on John during his recuperation for they were married eight days later, on February 18, 1751. Perhaps their haste was an effort to avoid Charles' interference again, for when told of their engagement he wrote, "Thunderstruck. I groaned all day, and several following ones, I could eat no pleasant food, nor preach, nor rest, either by night or by day."

For John Wesley, his marriage was to confirm the adage, "Marry in haste, repent in leisure." The new Mrs. Wesley proved herself extremely jealous, with a vile temper. One acquaintance, John Hampton, recounts an incident he witnessed while they were traveling in Ireland:

> Once I was on the point of committing murder. Once, when I was in the North of Ireland, I went into a room and found Mrs. Wesley foaming with fury. Her husband was on the floor, where she had been trailing him by the hair of his head; and she was still holding in her hand venerable locks which she had plucked up by the roots. I felt as though I could have knocked the soul out of her.

Over the years—to John's great relief—Mary Wesley deserted him a number of times. However, she always returned. Finally, in 1781, she died while John was on a preaching tour. "I came to London, and was informed that my wife died on Monday," he wrote tersely.

During the thirty years of his marriage, John Wesley was not completely occupied with placating the virago that he had wed and, one must admit, the life he had chosen must have been hard on his wife. He was constantly on the road preaching and when he was not preaching, he read and wrote voluminously. All told, besides the private writings of his journal and diary, he wrote 230 original works. John's life was devoted to Methodism and its dissemination; in many ways there was little room for another in his affections.

By the time of Mary Wesley's death, Methodism had spread throughout England and Ireland and captured not only the lower classes with its message, but the upper classes also, and had traveled across the ocean to the shores of the New World. Although there were Methodists in America, for the most part they were immigrants who had carried their worship with them, without the benefit of a preacher. At the Conference of 1769, however, the membership voted to send two preachers to America for a tour of preaching. The conference had been encouraged in this decision by the establishment of a Methodist chapel in New York in 1768.

On October 22, 1769, Richard Boardman and Joseph Pilmore arrived in Philadelphia to begin their American tour. Boardman, whose health was poor, spent most of his time in New York. Pilmore, younger and hardier, was able to do more. He established his ministry in Philadelphia and traveled extensively on the East Coast and in the South. Like Wesley, Pilmore was an organizer with definite thoughts of what Methodism ought to be.

He noted these in his journal. Among them were:

1. That the Methodist Society was never designed to make a Separation from the Church of England or be looked upon as a Church . . .
3. That any person who is so convinced and desires admittance into the Society, will readily be received as a probationer.

4. That those who walk according to the Oracles of God, and thereby give proof [of] their sincerity, will readily be admitted into full connexion with the Methodists.

5. That if any person or persons in the Society, walk *disorderly*, and transgress the holy laws of God, we will admonish him of his error . . . we will bear with him for a time, but if he remains incorrigible and impenetent, we must then of necessity inform him, he is no longer a member of the Society.

Pilmore's strengths, like Wesley's, were in preaching and organizing. By the time he departed for England in 1774, he had already made significant progress in establishing Methodist societies in America. Pilmore was to return to America several times, and his work was supplemented and continued by two men who arrived in America in 1771, Richard Wright and Francis Asbury. Francis Asbury would become known, because of the extent of his work and influence, as the "Wesley of America."

John Wesley was sympathetic with the work in America, feeling that here was fertile ground in which Methodism could grow, but he was puzzled by the colonists and their demands for freedom. Initially he was in favor of the cause of American independence and disapproved of the Crown's actions against the colonists, saying, "I doubt whether any man can defend them either on the foot of law, equity or prudence." In 1775, however, he published his *Calm Address to our American Colonies*, defending England's right to tax the colonists without representation, and in 1777 his even less tolerant *Calm Address to the Inhabitants of England* was published, in which he roundly denounced the rebelling colonists.

With the end of the American Revolution, Wesley once again saw opportunity in America. As he had earlier proclaimed, "the world is my parish," and the New World needed more support than had previously been given. Accordingly, in 1784 he approached the bishop of London with a request for a number of preachers to be ordained and sent to America. The bishop refused and, in September of 1784, John Wesley himself ordained Dr. Thomas Coke to the office of Superintendent of the Societies in America, at the same time ordaining two others as presbyters. Their ordination enabled Dr. Coke and the others to give the sacraments; John Wesley had broken the Methodist ties with the Church of England.

Considering that all his life John Wesley had stressed that the Methodists were merely to be societies within the larger structure of the Church of England, it would seem that he was contradicting all that he had preached. Yet his actions were not inconsistent with his philosophy. To his way of thinking, "Insofar as institutions stifled the possibility of man's response [to God's sanctifying grace], to that extent they stifled the grace of God and supporting institutions must be allowed to suppliment their deficiency."[1] If the church, by stifling the supporting institutions, thereby denied man the possibility of experiencing God's grace, then the church must be abandoned. What was of overwhelming importance to John Wesley were not the institutions of man, but providing man with the opportunity for salvation.

The same year that John ordained Coke as a minister, the conference, then referred to as the Legal Hundred, also passed the Deed of Declaration of 1784, which represented yet another break from the traditions of the Church of England. The deed gave the conference the authority to appoint a successor to Wesley after his death, removing that power from the church. This revolt was followed, in 1787, with the licensing of Methodist chapels. The Methodists were now an independent denomination.

John had planned for Charles to succeed him as head of the Methodist movement on his death, but Charles died in 1788. He left two sons, both gifted musicians, who were strongly opposed to the Methodist way of life; one, in fact, became a Roman Catholic.

John remained hale and hearty until his death in 1791. As he wrote in 1790, "I am now an old man, decayed from head to foot. . . . However, blessed be God, I do not slack my labour. *I can preach and write still.*" His ways remained the same, his days spent traveling, reading, and preaching. The only concession he made to age was that he traveled by carriage rather than on horseback.

In March of 1791 John became weak and took to his bed. It is reported that his last hours were peaceful and, as he died, he proclaimed, "The best of all is—God is with us!" On the second of March 1791, John Wesley passed away, leaving an institution that had been and continues to be a force of religious and social reform both in England and America and—in later years— around the world.

At the time of his death, Wesley little realized the

changes that would occur within his beloved Methodism, although in America Methodists had already begun to follow their own path. Their leader on that path was Francis Asbury.

VIII

Gathering Souls in America

FRANCIS ASBURY WAS ONLY TWENTY-FOUR YEARS OLD when he arrived in America with Richard Wright in 1771. At the time of his arrival, there were approximately 600 Methodists in the colonies. "Two years later there were 1,160. Three years after this in 1776 . . . there were 4,921; in 1786, 20,689; and in 1800 there were 63,958."[1] This dramatic growth in so short a time was due, in large part, to the tireless efforts of Asbury.

Asbury was the son of a Staffordshire tenant farmer and a Welshwoman who had only the highest ambitions for her son. Like the others who came to America before him, Asbury was a lay preacher. Appointed by Wesley, he was preceded by Robert Williams around

1768; Richard Boardman and Joseph Pilman in 1769; and, after them, in the same year, John King. In addition to the official evangelists—those sent by Wesley—there were a great number of unauthorized laymen who chose to spread the word. These tended to be troublesome to the official ministers, but there was very little they could do to control them. One of the best known was a former Irishman, Robert Strawbridge of Maryland.

After establishing himself in the northern part of Maryland near Sam's Creek, Strawbridge built himself a large log cabin and, around 1764, began preaching and conducting classes; it is speculated that his were the first Methodist classes in America. Francis Asbury notes, "Here Mr. Strawbridge formed the first society in Maryland—and *America*."

Strawbridge was to be a continual problem to Asbury and the other early evangelists. Although they were firmly under the control of John Wesley, Strawbridge was fiercely independent and did as he pleased. Neither a lay preacher nor an ordained minister, Strawbridge began preaching "because he recognized a need."[2] Shortly thereafter he began administering the sacraments of baptism and the Holy Supper. The preachers sent by Wesley were horrified. The bestowal of the sacraments was the province of the Anglican church alone.

At the first conference of preachers in America in 1774, the debate over administering the sacraments was furious. To many, who were loyal to the colonists' call for revolution, the issue represented the domination of England. Wesley's decrees prevailed, however, and the conference issued a statement saying that no one should administer the sacraments. Asbury wryly added in his journal, however, "except Mr. Strawbridge, and he under the particular direction of the assistant [Thomas Rankin]."

In 1773, John Wesley had sent two more lay preachers to the colonies, Thomas Rankin and George Shadford. He appointed Rankin general assistant for America. Rankin was sent to bring order to the movement in America and Asbury noted of him, "He will not be admired as a preacher. But as a disciplinarian he will fill his place." Rankin and Asbury, two very different types of men, were to butt heads more than once, including over what to do about Robert Strawbridge.

Even the rigid Thomas Rankin could not curtail Strawbridge. A meeting was held in Maryland and, as Asbury wrote in his journal, "I read part of our minutes, to see if brother Strawbridge would conform; but he appeared to be inflexible. He would not administer the ordinances under our direction at all." It was some relief to the English preachers when Strawbridge died in 1781. Asbury said, "He is now no more; upon the whole, I am inclined to think the Lord took him away in judgement, because he was in a way to do hurt to his cause."

While Strawbridge's group may have been the first Methodist society in America, more important to the history of American Methodism were his attitudes. His fierce independence was something new in the movement, and the well-disciplined evangelists from Britain were at a loss as to how to deal with it. Reared beneath the cloak of John Wesley, Asbury and the other English preachers did not know what to do with those who, having experienced a justification of faith similar to

Wesley's, then felt obliged by Christ to preach—without the blessing or approval of either John Wesley or the Church of England. It is, in hindsight, a movement that is only to be expected in a land where, at the time, the idea of freedom, and religious freedom in particular, were being so widely discussed. When Asbury arrived in 1771, Wesley's organization of societies and conferences was loosely in place, but there were also a great many small churches led by lay ministers who had to be brought more closely into the traditional structure. Against the background of the Revolutionary War (1775–1783), his task was doubly hard.

As John Wesley had done before him, Francis Asbury took up reins as an itinerant preacher, traveling prodigiously to spread the word and to organize. All his life he would stress the value of itinerancy, forcing all who came within his province to take to the road also. A James Quinn, who traveled with Asbury for a while, recalled an incident in which an old woman asked Asbury where he lived, to which he replied,

> No foot of land do I possess
>   No cottage in this wilderness,
>   A poor way-faring man.
>   I lodge awhile in tents below,
>   Or gladly wander to and fro,
>   Till I my Canaan gain.
>
>   Nothing on earth I call my own,
>   A stranger to the world unknown
>   I all their goods despise;
>   I trample on their whole delight,
>   And seek a city out of sight,
>   A city in the skies.[3]

Asbury felt the role of the itinerant preacher to be a key one. This idea, too, would be challenged in the new land of America.

Joseph Pilmore was one of those who had come to disagree with the need for ceaseless traveling. He complained, both to others and in his journal, that it was unsettling. Richard Boardman, with whom he had traveled to America, kept insisting that they regularly exchange places; Boardman was in New York, Pilmore in Philadelphia. "Frequent changes," Pilmore wrote, "amongst gospel preachers, may keep up the spirits of some kinds of people, but is never likely to promote the spirit of the Gospel nor increase true religion." Asbury tried to counter such arguments by example, traveling further and more frequently than almost any preacher had before him.

As the Revolutionary War loomed nearer, many of the British preachers found themselves in uncomfortable positions. The Methodists avowed their loyalty to the Church of England, which angered many colonists; and they were not helped by their founder, John Wesley, writing and preaching against such a revolution. One by one, Wesley's British preachers returned to England or fled to Canada. Those who remained tried to carry on as best they could. On the very eve of the revolution, the third Annual Conference met in May 1775, in Philadelphia where, at the same time, the Second Continental Congress was meeting.

The Methodists were caught in a volley of conflicting sentiments. The Americans were calling for a severance of ties with England, and the Wesleys were attacking the Americans. Charles, for example, wrote of them, "Ye vipers who your Parent tear/With evil all our good requite." As Rankin was to comment, "How difficult to stand in such a situation, and not be blamed by violent men on both sides."

By 1778 all who had been sent by John Wesley from England had left America, except Francis Asbury. Asbury, as Wesley's sole representative, was now general assistant. He was finding his job a difficult one, however, because of the increased restrictions on travel within the colonies and on the enforcement of a loyalty oath. Some of the loyalty oaths also required one to serve in the military. Asbury, who was opposed to all violence, found it harder and harder to evade the oath. Finally he settled in Kent County, Delaware, at the home of Judge Thomas White, a good Methodist. In Delaware the oath was not as harsh as elsewhere. George Roberts, one contemporary of Asbury's, wrote of his time there,

> Mr. White was a magistrate and a gentleman of influence and he did everything to make his [Asbury's] life comfortable. Here he was hid like the prophet of Israel and he poured out his soul to God for the prosperity of Zion, and the peace of the world—and looked with solicitude for the time when he could go forth unrestrained and offer once more salvation upon the whole of the Gospel.[4]

But Asbury had gained a reputation—all Methodists were suspect because of their allegiance to the Church of England. Shortly after his arrival at White's, White was arrested on suspicion of having ties to Asbury, who when the soldiers approached had hidden in a nearby swamp. White was shortly released, and Asbury returned to White's home. There he stayed until 1780.

Because it was so difficult for Asbury to travel, and because the other preachers from England had fled, Methodism fell into the hands of American preachers. Foreseeing this situation, they had initially voted to continue following the direction of John Wesley and his preachers. At the Annual Conference of 1777, the native preachers drew up and signed a document of their intentions:

> We, whose names are underwritten, being thoroughly convinced of the necessity of a close union between those whom God hath used as instruments in his glorious work, in order to preserve this union, are resolved, God being our helper, 1. To devote ourselves to God, taking up our cross daily, steadily aiming at this one thing, to save our souls and them that hear us. 2. To preach the old Methodist doctrine, and no other, as contained in the Minutes. 3. To observe and enforce the whole Methodist Discipline, as laid down in the said Minutes. 4. To choose a committee of assistants to transact the business that is now done by the general assistants, and the old preachers who come from Britain.

Asbury was among the signers of this resolution and, perhaps realizing that he would have to go into hiding because of the political climate, offered no objections to, in essense, turning over the official reins of American Methodism to the "native" preachers. Getting them back, however, would require all his abundant tact and diplomacy.

Most of the native preachers and lay members of Methodism supported the Revolution. But because of their ties with Anglicanism, they still fell under as much suspicion as those who had definite Tory sympathies. One difficulty lay in the fact that many were conscientious objectors, although Methodism did not actively encourage this stance. Many felt that they had no role at all to play in politics. One such was William Watters, a Methodist preacher:

> I firmly believed my business was to preach the Gospel, and not to meddle with those public affairs, which were in much better hands, and in my opinion was unbecoming men of my profession.

For every Methodist who refused to fight, however, there was another to prove his loyalty on the battlefield.

While the Methodists were torn over taking up arms in the wars, they faced another conflict within their ranks. Hitherto the sacraments had been taken in the Anglican Church. With the Revolution, the American Anglican Church almost totally collapsed. Most of its clergy fled the country; others were imprisoned on suspicion of being spies. Where then were the Methodists to go for the sacraments? At the Annual Conference of 1779 held in Fluvanna County, Virginia, this was the primary topic of concern, and one that would cause a temporary split among the American Methodists.

One segment of the Methodists advocated the status quo, declaring that nothing should be done or changed until John Wesley advised them. The opposing group insisted that the current situation warranted providing the sacraments to their parishioners themselves. By saying this, they were denying the authority of Asbury as general assistant and also changing their relationship to the Church of England. The split in opinion tended to follow geographical lines.

Prior to the Fluvanna conference, a group of northern preachers had met with Asbury at White's house and confirmed him as leader, voting to delay for a year any decision on whether to assure the authority of the Anglican church and ordain preachers. The Fluvanna meeting was attended primarily by southern preachers with only William Watters there as a northern observer. Ignoring a written plea from Asbury, they voted to set up a presbytery of four ministers who would ordain each other and then ordain other preachers as needed, to administer the sacraments—an idea more Baptist in philosophy than Methodist.

This move by the southern Methodists was abhorrent to the northern Methodists. In 1780 they met and voted a denunciation of the southerners' decision, stating that they were not to be called Methodists "till they come back." Asbury, Garrettson, and Watters traveled to deliver this message in person and to seek to change the minds of the southern leaders. They initially refused, but finally, drawing on his extensive powers of diplomacy, Asbury got them to agree not to act until John Wesley could send his opinion. When Wesley did write, he strongly supported Asbury, and the southern Methodists agreed to abide by his decision.

Although the rift was healed, it was an indication of the different perspectives held by American Methodists and British Methodists. Far away from the personal influence and magnetism of John Wesley, the Americans tended to question his advice and authority, and anti-British sentiment eroded it further. A new kind of Methodism was evolving, one that was uniquely American.

With the American group, however, dissent had raised its head. This too was very American. In Britain, decisions were made by John Wesley and a council of elders, with Wesley having the final say; no one questioned those decisions. In America, decisions were questioned. This would lead, in the years to come, to arguments, some easily solved, some long-lasting, that would threaten to disrupt the whole fabric of American Methodism at times. However, until 1816, when he died, Francis Asbury managed to keep Methodism in America on an even keel, through insightful management and by setting an example of zealous hard work that few could question—or emulate.

IX

"So Easily Are Bishops Made"

IN 1784 JOHN WESLEY ORDAINED DR. THOMAS COKE AS superintendent of the societies of America, an office Coke was to share with Francis Asbury. "I can by no means agree," Wesley wrote, "to leave such a field for gathering souls to Christ as we have in America. . . . Therefore I am determined by the Grace of God, not to leave them, let the consequences be what it may."

While American Methodists were jubilant, British Methodists were uneasy—some even angry. Charles Wesley, who generally followed his brother in all things, was outraged. He expressed his shock in a hymn that is not included in the Methodist hymnbooks.

So easily are Bishops made
 by man's, or woman's whim?
 W———— his hands on C———— hath laid,
  But who laid hands on Him?

Hands on himself he laid, and took
 An Apostolic Chair:
And then ordain'd his Creature C————
 His Heir and Successor.

Episcopalians, now no more
 With Presbyterians fight,
But give your needless Contest o'er,
 'Whose Ordination's right?

It matters not, if Both are One,
 Or different in degree,
For lo! ye see contain'd in John
 The whole Presbytery![1]

Dr. Coke arrived in America on November 3, 1784, and, meeting with Asbury on November 14, told him of the honor he had been told to bestow upon him: ordination as bishop and superintendent. To his surprise, Asbury would act only if the American preachers voted him to the office: "If the preachers unanimously choose me, I shall not accept in the capacity I have hitherto done by Mr. Wesley's appointment." To that purpose, Asbury called for a conference to meet on December 24 in Baltimore; in the meantime he sent Dr. Coke out as an itinerant preacher.

Known as the Christmas Conference, the meeting held at Perry Hall just outside of Baltimore essentially established Methodism as a new "church"—a denomination—in the United States. At the meeting, Dr. Coke presented an abridged Articles of Religion adapted from the Thirty-Nine Articles of the Anglican church, "a revised Sunday Service based on the *Book of Common Prayer*, ordination certificates authenticating Wesley's action, . . . and a general letter to the preachers in America."[2] With these and the *Large Minutes*, one of the Books of Discipline that governs each branch of Methodists, the Americans had everything they needed to function as a denomination. As John Wesley had written, "We judge it best that they should stand fast in that liberty wherewith God has so strangely made them free."

The documents were received and the ordination of Francis Asbury was proposed to the members of the conference. The members voted unanimously for the idea and over the next three days Asbury was ordained deacon, elder, and superintendent of the Episcopal Methodist Church of America, so named because it intended to maintain the traditions of the Anglican (Episcopal) church but be Methodist in orientation. At the same time, a number of others were ordained as elders. They then turned their attention to another matter, the creation of a college at Abingdon, Maryland, to be named Cokesbury College in honor of Coke and Asbury (an immodest move for which John Wesley would chastise both Coke and Asbury).

Since the first preachers had been sent from England in the 1760s, the structure of Methodism introduced into America was the same one that Wesley had devised in 1739. As he wrote in *The Nature, Design and*

General Rules of the United States, in London, Bristol, Kingswood, Newcastle-upon-Tyne, &c., 1743, the organization was based on the concept of Societies.

> Such a society is no other than "a company of men having the form and seeking the power of godliness, united in order to pray together, to receive the word of exhortation, and to watch over one another in love, that they may help each other to work out their salvation."
>   . . . each society is divided into smaller companies called *classes.* . . . There are about twelve persons in every class; one of whom is styled *the leader.* It is his business. (1) To see each person in his class once a week at least, in order to inquire how their souls prosper; to advise, reprove, comfort, or exhort, as occasion may require; to receive what they are willing to give toward the relief of the poor. (b) To meet the Minister and the Stewards of the society once a week. . . .

Up until 1784 American Methodists had met together in societies and classes and, sometimes in a chapel, to hear the itinerant preachers. To receive the sacraments, they joined with the Anglican Church. After 1784 there was at times some confusion. The traveling preacher was a full member of the annual conference, while the local preacher, whether ordained or not, was only authorized to preach in the town or county in which he lived and was not a member of the annual conference; he usually could not give the sacraments. Becoming a local preacher, however, was one of the first steps toward ordination and eventually becoming a member of the conference by assuming the duties of the itinerant preacher. But the local preacher was in a sort of limbo, being neither layman nor clergy, and this led to some discontent.

As the years passed, more and more itinerant preachers were becoming local pastors, thereby losing their conference membership. The traveling life was hard and, although there was no explicit rule about it, the preachers were expected to remain unmarried, as Wesley had been for much of his life and as Francis Asbury still was. When thought of marriage entered a preacher's mind, he would often voluntarilay give up traveling to marry and raise a family. Sometimes marriage was not even a factor. Many preachers found towns or areas that they liked on their travels and decided to settle down. But when they did so, they no longer had a part in the decision-making of the church in their region.

In 1792, finding that it was difficult to govern through annual conferences alone, Asbury and Coke had set up the general conference to meet every four years. At the General Conference of 1796, six geographically defined annual conferences had been established, one of which was the open-ended, or regional, Western Conference covering the territories of the Western frontier. And in 1808, the general conference approved a "plan for a *delegated* general conference with a constitutional basis of authority . . . which prevails in the council of United Methodists [i.e., Modern Methodists] to this day."[3] The criterion for membership, however, continued to be whether or not a preacher was an itinerant.

While local preachers had the advantage of knowing their parishioners well and being able to care for their specific needs, the traveling preacher also benefited the

Methodists. Not only did he hold revivals which brought new members to the church, but his arrival in a town was a special event and jogged those who were already Methodists out of any complacency into which they may have sunk. The traveling preacher was a tie among all the smaller groups in a region, and between them and the annual conference. Traveling preachers were assigned their circuits at the annual conference and rotated regions. In this way, not only did the local people get fresh viewpoints, the preachers were able to use their sermons several times over. But there were rumbles of discontent with this system. More and more of the local preachers—particularly if they had previously been itinerant—wished to have a say at the conferences; the lay people wanted representation.

Another source of discontent was the fact that itinerancy was grueling. Many itinerants complained to Asbury about the conditions under which they had to travel and preach. One contemporary of Asbury's, George Roberts, wrote of Asbury,

> In every case he could say I have labored more abundantly than you all—He would frequently be on horseback at sunrise, travel fifteen or twenty miles to breakfast and not put up till nine and ten o'clock at night— He would . . . say to the preachers when complaining of their hardships, "You must have a stomach for every man's table and a back for every man's bed—that the cause was His who said to His disciples when He was with them in the flesh, *The foxes have holes and the birds of the air have nests but the Son of Man has nowhere to lay His head.*"

During Asbury's lifetime he managed to quell any calls

for reforms, but after his death in 1816 the cries became louder and there was no strong leader such as Asbury to calm them. It all came to a head at the General Conference of 1820.

By 1820, the quadrennial general conference had superceded the annual conference in handling matters on a national level. Up until Asbury's death he presided over both the conference and the church in general as bishop, with a committee of elders of his choosing. It had been suggested several times that the elders be elected by the traveling preachers attending the conference, but Asbury had managed to avoid this issue in his lifetime. By 1820, however, it could no longer be ignored.

During the second week of the Conference of 1820, a motion was put forward to elect presiding elders. This was hotly debated and a compromise motion was proposed "which restricted the election to nominees, three times the number needed, submitted by Bishops."[4] This motion was passed by the majority and all seemed comfortable with the idea, but then Joshua Soule stepped in.

Joshua Soule was a determined leader with very definite ideas. During the conference he had been elected bishop, but now he refused to assume office if the motion on elected elders was implemented. Surprisingly, after several days of furious debate, the conference voted not to put the motion into action. Many were dissatisfied. One, Nicholas Snethen, wrote,

When our countrymen find every idea which they have been in the habit of attaching to a constitution reversed, and instead of this instrument being a palladium of

liberty, as they supposed, becoming a mere charter of
self-created and monopolized power, must they not lose
all confidence in the agents who produced the transfor-
mation.[5]

This dissent was to brew over the next eight years and
erupt in 1828, resulting in bitterness and division.

During the period between 1820 and 1828, cries for
reform grew louder and stronger. In 1824 a protest at
the Baltimore conference gave rise to a number of
"union" societies, Methodist societies united in their
drive for reform. The official publication of the Methodists, the *Methodist Magazine,* refused to print any of
the arguments calling for reform and, to fill the void, a
number of other publications arose. Among these were
the *Wesleyan Repository and Religious Intelligencer,*
and *Mutual Rights.* Then, in 1827, Alexander McCaine
published his *History and Mystery of Methodist Epis-
copacy,* which became a rallying point for the reformers. In it he held that the office of bishop was not and
never was intended by John Wesley to be all-powerful,
but rather, was meant to be a third form of ministry.
"The present form of government," he wrote, "was sur-
reptitiously introduced and was imposed upon the societies under the sanction of Mr. Wesley's name." There
needed to be a system of control, he suggested, check-
ing the potentially limitless power then given the
bishop. This publication aroused much debate and controversy.

Meanwhile, those who espoused the cause of reform
were being suspended or expelled from their conferences and their churches for their ideas. In 1827 they

gathered together in Baltimore for the first General Convention of Reformers and prepared a statement to be presented at the General Conference of 1828. It called for the reforms discussed and an end to the persecution of those who advocated those measures.

When this document was presented at the General Conference of 1828, it was soundly rejected and its authors chastised. The only concession made was a motion submitted by John Emory, which offered reinstatement to those reformers who denounced their views. There were not many takers, however.

One result of this controversy was the decision by the union societies to hold their own conference, and in November of 1828 the Associated Methodist Churches met, marking one step toward the formation of a separate denomination. Other groups followed and in 1830 the Methodist Protestant Church was organized. This denomination did away with the office of bishop altogether; authority resided in the president of the annual conference, subject to "revision by a Committee of Appeals."

Because of internal strife and, in some instances, shear hardheadedness, the "connection" that John Wesley had envisioned seemed to be crumbling in America. While British Methodists continued to follow steadily in Wesley's footsteps, the American Methodists were taking up the concepts embodied in the United States Constitution and demanding equality, representation, and democracy in their churches. When these were not forthcoming, they went their own ways to form separate churches.

While 1828 marked the first definite schism within

the Methodist Church in America, it did not mark the first "separation" of churches within Methodism. That had already occurred with the segregation of blacks and whites.

X

Souls to Save

WHEN NEGRO SLAVERY WAS INTRODUCED INTO NORTH America, little thought was given then or after, to a slave's physical comfort, much less to his or her spiritual well-being. Not only were the few evangelical and missionizing groups more concerned with increasing the number of members from their own race, but most preached a religion alien to the slave's own experience. In many African religions there was "no sharp delineation between the sacred and the secular. . . . The Africans saw life as a whole; it was a unity."[1] The extreme Calvinist doctrine of the Puritans, and the teachings of the early Anglican church and others in the seventeenth and eighteenth centuries, often excluded blacks from among those who could be saved, although it was felt that exposure to religion—Christian religion—

might have a beneficial influence. Most evangelists did not try to abolish the institution of slavery, but did try to ameliorate its appalling conditions.

One such was George Whitefield. He approved of slavery and kept slaves himself. But he believed that blacks could be saved and that this would enable the slave to transcend all "earthly conditions and sufferings."[2] In 1748, however, Whitefield urged the colony of Georgia to adopt slavery; when John Wesley had traveled there slavery was forbidden. Although Whitefield chastised cruel slaveowners, he also felt that the Georgia colony would not prosper without slavery. He seemed to have no trouble juggling religion and slavery, and this was yet another point of disagreement between Wesley and him.

In the late eighteenth century things changed spiritually for both free and enslaved blacks. During that time various Protestant sects began actively evangelizing among blacks and advocating abolition. Most notable among these were the Methodists. The Methodists had great appeal for the poor and laboring classes in both Britain and America because of their idea that, through faith and devotion, anybody could be saved, and because of John Wesley's emphasis on good works. It was only natural for the Methodists in America to turn their attentions to the enslaved and abused. Unlike other evangelists, Methodist preachers were concerned with the physical as well as the religious health of the blacks in America. Methodists openly condemned slavery and called for its abolition. John Wesley himself had prayed for an end to slavery and supported those who fought against it. In 1791, just before his death, Wesley wrote to William Wilberforce, supporting his abolitionist efforts:

If God be for you, who can be against you? Are all of
them [the advocates of slavery] together stronger than
God? . . . Go on, in the name of God and in the power of
his might, till even American slavery (the vilest that
ever saw the sun) shall vanish away before.

Wesley's comments were echoed by Asbury, Coke, and
later leaders of the church.

Methodism provided the black slave both with a
hope for spiritual salvation and a hope for freedom.
Methodists also tried to ease the sorrows of the blacks
by good works, material donations, and money. Like
many African religions, Methodism united the secular
and the sacred. The result was only to be expected. The
Methodists had great success converting both free and
enslaved blacks. By 1816 there were 42,304 black members of the Methodist Church, and in 1844 that number
had risen to 145,409.[3] This is, however, a small number
when one considers that by 1860 there were three million slaves in the United States and an unknown
number of free blacks.

The emotionalism of early Methodism had attracted
many in Britain, Ireland, and Wales, and it had similar
appeal to American blacks when first evangelized by
itinerant preachers. In 1776 Thomas Rankin, a Methodist preacher, "had to pause in the midst of his sermon on the prophetic vision of the valley of dry bones,
to beg his hearers to compose themselves. 'But they
would not,' he says; 'some on their knees, some on
their faces crying mightily to God all the time I was
preaching. Hundreds of Negroes were among them with
tears streaming down their faces.' "[4]

Upon conversion, blacks were initially accepted into
the white churches and societies without distinction as

to color, but segregation soon reared its head. Often black church members were forced to sit in the balconies or at the back of churches, or attend separate services. This led some Negroes, especially in the North, to withdraw and form their own congregations, and later their own denominations. Sometimes such discrimination was unwitting, sometimes with intent. One Benjamin Abbott described a meeting he attended:

> We soon fell into conversation on the things of God. At time of family worship, abundance of black people assembled in the kitchen, and a door was set open that they might hear without coming into the parlor.

Although early segregation was often instituted without thought, after 1784 and the formation of Methodism into a denomination, segregation became conscious and widespread, especially in the South, and resentment was building. One early black leader, Richard Allen of Philadelphia, told of an experience he had when he and several friends attended St. George's Church. Finding no seats in the "black" section, they tried to sit in the "white" section. They were then attacked by the sexton and physically pushed and shoved out of the church. This was too much for Allen, so he and a number of other black Methodists started their own church in Philadelphia. When the elders of St. George's Church objected strenuously,

> We told him we had no place of worship, and we did not mean to go to St. George's any more, as we were so scandalously treated in presence of all the congregation present; "and if you deny us your name, you cannot seal up the Scriptures from us, and deny us a name in

heaven. We believe heaven is free for all who worship in spirit and truth."[5]

Richard Allen and his followers were able to organize their own church in 1794, despite opposition, and Francis Asbury opened their "house for Divine service." Allen's church and the few other black groups which had broken away from their white churches, faced increasing pressure to be brought under the auspices of the general conference. This they wished to avoid, because of past grievances and a desire for autonomy. Finally, on April 9, 1816, Richard Allen, Daniel Coker, and James Champion called a meeting of black church leaders:

> Delegates from Baltimore and other places met those from Philadelphia and taking into consideration their grievances, and in order to secure their privileges, promote union and harmony among themselves, it was resolved, "that the people of Philadelphia, Baltimore, etc., etc., should become one body, under the name of the African Methodist Episcopal Church, A.M.E."

Following the Methodist practice, Richard Allen, widely known as Father Allen, was elected bishop to head the new denomination, with a council of elders, through the system of annual conferences.

The A.M.E. Church was the first to ordain black elders and a black Methodist bishop. This opened an avenue of opportunity to blacks at a time when opportunity was sadly lacking. Within the church, blacks had the chance to advance. While black lay preachers had been recruited into the traditional Methodist Episcopal church and black preachers had been ordained, that was as far as these men could go; there was no hope of ever attaining the rank of elder or bishop. For this reason, among others, the A. M. E. Church grew rapidly, in two years increasing its membership six-fold and expanding geographically as well.

The development of the African Methodist Episcopal Zion Church, like that of the A.M.E. Church, also stemmed from dissatisfaction over segregation. It met with few of the problems that the A. M. E. Church encountered, however. Founded in New York City, its members originally were members of the John Street Church, the first Methodist chapel in America.

The development of the A.M.E.Z. Church was gradual. As the John Street Church grew from its founding in 1768, its black membership also increased. As in other churches, blacks were segregated, but the John Street Church presented a special problem because of its size; it was quite small and a number of whites expressed dissatisfaction at having to sit so close to those of an inferior class or even slaves. In addition, many of the black members felt that the services did not speak to their condition or needs. They felt that this could perhaps be remedied by having occasional prayer meetings by themselves. In 1780 the New York Annual Conference posed the question,

> Ought not the assistant [Francis Asbury] to meet the colored people himself, and appoint in his absence proper white persons, and not suffer them to stay so late and meet by themselves?
> Answer: Yes

The conference granted the black church members the

right to meet separately, under the guidance of a duly appointed white official.

As the meetings became more popular, they started taking on the characteristics of a service, including preaching as well as prayers. There were several black preachers attached to the John Street Church, but since the New York conference, after 1784, refused to ordain them as deacons or elders, they could not give the sacraments. The reasons given by the conference for refusing ordination were lack of education and the inability of black preachers to travel freely as Methodist itinerants were required to do. During slavery, any black seen traveling without his master, or a pass from his master, could be detained as a runaway.

By 1796 the John Street Church was having difficulty keeping up with its members. There were so many that it was difficult to fit everyone—black or white—into the church for services. The church also complained that the separate meetings with the blacks were overtaking the white ministers. That year a group of black ministers met with Bishop Asbury to try to reach an accommodation. Among them were those who would later found the A.M.E. Zion denomination: Francis Jacobs, William Brown, Peter Williams, Abraham Thompson, and June Scott. After discussion, Asbury gave them permission to meet "in the interval of the regular preaching hours of our white brethren," and to hold services "in the best manner they could." This was merely a temporary solution, and it did not solve the long-term overcrowding problem at John Street Church.

In a further attempt to remedy the overcrowding, the black members set up a chapel in a nearby cabinet-maker's shop. Fitted with seats, a pulpit and a balcony, it became an extension of John Street Church and was known as the African Chapel. Prayer meetings were held three times a week, and services were conducted by Abraham Thompson, William Miller, or June Scott, or by a visiting preacher. For the sacraments, however, members still had to crowd into the John Street Church.

After several years, even the African Chapel could not easily hold all the black congregation. This time, however, its members sought a more permanent solution: the establishment of a new church "under the Methodist government." Unlike Richard Allen in Philadelphia, they encountered no opposition to the idea from either the John Street Church or the New York Conference. Money was raised and a church building erected at Leonard and Church streets in New York. The members named it Zion, although its official name was the African Methodist Episcopal Church called Zion. An agreement was drawn up that firmly anchored the new church to the Methodist church, although one issue was left unresolved—ordination.

The new church grew quickly. It was not without problems, however. Funds were short and preachers poorly paid. In 1813 Thomas Sipkins, who had been criticized by Zion leaders for "headstrong" behavior, broke away and started his own church, also under Methodist auspices. The new church, Asbury Church, developed its own congregation and functioned smoothly in its relations with Zion Church. There was no thought on the part of either to break away from the parent Methodist Episcopal Church, and those who occasionally mentioned the idea were sharply rebuked. Richard Allen met the same reaction when he attempted to establish the A.M.E. in New York. They already had a church, they told him; they did not need his renegade bunch.

The issue of the role of the black member in the Methodist Church arose at around the same time that the church was being criticized for a lack of reform, and for many of the same reasons. On the local level, the New York churches, black and white, both wished for more representation at the New York Annual Conference, and a greater voice in forming the Discipline, the set of rules by which each Methodist lived. They also felt that the Board of Trustees for the churches in New York City were showing favoritism. The Board of Trustees managed all the churches' property communally and it seemed to many that John Street Church was being favored at the expense of the others. These complaints culminated in 1820 when the Reverend William Stillwell, an elder in charge of the Zion and Asbury churches, petitioned the New York conference for relief. When he was rejected, Stillwell and a number of others walked out of the meeting. Stillwell lost his appointments to the two churches as a result of his actions but, more importantly, this brought into the open many of the complaints harbored by black members, particularly regarding ordination.

Although they still considered themselves linked to the Methodist Episcopal Church, by 1820 the Zion and Asbury churches realized they could do little more than form their own denomination. With Stillwell removed, there was none, black or white, to give the sacraments, and the conference still refused to ordain black ministers to do so. The only way they could advance their own churches was to withdraw. This they did, with Abraham Thompson serving as president of the annual meeting. They rewrote the Disicpline to suit their own needs and ruled that elders could be elected by the congregation and could then administer the sacraments. In 1828 what is regarded as the first General Conference of the African Methodist Episcopal Zion Church Connection met in New York City, with Christopher Rush elected general superintendent.

Unlike the A.M.E. Church, the A.M.E.Z. Church grew slowly in its first years, garnering few memberships outside of New York. The A.M.E. Church, or "Allenites," had a head start on them and many black churches were already affiliated with it. As the A.M.E.Z. Church began evangelizing and preaching against slavery, however, its numbers steadily swelled. By 1860, on the eve of the Civil War, the A.M.E.Z. Church had 4,600 members and 105 preachers, of which 85 were elders.

A third black denomination grew up in Wilmington, Delaware, shunning the Allenites. Named the African Union Church (originally the Union Church of Africans), it was Methodist in orientation but its ministers were chosen by the congregations, and its ruling officer was called president rather than bishop. After the Civil War it was to merge with an offshoot of the A.M.E. Church, resulting in the formation of the African Union First Colored Methodist Protestant Church of the United States of America or Elsewhere.

The troubles within the Methodist Episcopal Church reflected those of the larger world around it. Just as, earlier, the Methodists in America had raised a cry for liberty and equality within the conferences, so too, in the mid-1800s, did they become a microcosm of the troubles that surrounded them. Slavery and the rights of man were the hotly debated topics of the day. Just as these issues were dividing the United States, so too would they divide the church.

XI

War and Separation

WHEN THE METHODIST LEADERS GATHERED FOR THE GEN-
eral Conference of 1844 at Greene Street Church in New
York City, although debate was expected, its results
were not anticipated. On the surface, the preachers had
come to discuss the authority of the General Conference and the "integrity of the episcopal office of
bishop."[1] Beneath this, the argument concerned the
issue of slavery.

Early on, the Methodist Church, following John
Wesley's sentiments, had condemned slavery and a rule
banning it had been inserted in the Discipline. In 1780,
the conference had voted in the affirmative on the questions:

Does this conference acknowledge that slavery is contrary to the laws of God, man, and nature, and hurtful to society, contrary to the dictates of conscience and pure religion, and doing that which we would not others should do us and ours?—Do we pass our disapprobation on all our friends who keep slaves, and advise their freedom?

The Christmas Conference of 1784 had gone further, requiring its members, with exceptions, to free their slaves. Various of the regional annual conferences had also passed resolutions condemning slavery. Overall, the official stance of the Methodist Episcopal Church was anti-slavery and pro-abolition.

While their hearts were in the right places, reality was a different matter for the Methodists, as for many at that time. Many Methodists did, indeed, free their slaves but an equal number still retained slaves and, for the most part, defiance of the church's resolutions went unpunished. The primary effect of such resolutions was to anger southern members of the church.

At the 1844 conference, however, matters took a different turn. Slavery again raised its head, but this time action replaced mere words. The Baltimore Annual Conference had suspended a Francis Harding for failing to free some slaves whom he had obtained by marriage. He appealed this decision to the General Conference, but the General Conference rejected his appeal, 117 to 56, only the southerners voting in his favor. The real test case was yet to come, however.

At this time the church had five bishops: Joshua Soule, Elijah Hedding, James O. Andrew, Thomas A. Morris, and Beverly Waugh. Of these, Andrew was from Georgia and Waugh from Virginia; the others came from northern states. Bishop James Andrew was a slaveholder and the General Conference now turned to consider his status.

Andrew had inherited two slaves from his first wife, and his second wife owned several. As Georgia law forbade the emancipation of slaves, Andrew could not free them. In his defense, he pointed out that he had never bought or sold a slave, and his position was only that of trustee. Initially a resolution was proposed that he resign his office. This led to fierce debate out of which came the compromise resolution that he "desist from the exercise of this office so long as this impediment remains." The vote was 110 to 68, again splitting along geographical lines, with the southerners outvoted by the northerners. The debate and the following vote made it clear to the General Conference that the church might soon separate along north-south lines. A Committee of Nine was formed to work on a plan of separation, in case such an event occurred.

The Plan of Separation was presented to the General Conference on June 8th. It made provision for the establishment of a boundary between the north and south churches (similar to the Mason-Dixon line). Individual churches along the dividing line were permitted to decide their allegience by majority vote. Ministers were given the power to choose for themselves. The plan also provided for the equal distribution of publishing houses and recognized the validity of the Methodist Episcopal Church, South, should it be formed.

While the Plan of Separation was merely a scheme to be implemented in the event of separation, few doubted that the hours put into devising it would be wasted, and their expectations were soon realized. Less than a year later, southern delegates called for a general conference of their own to discuss constitutional issues in Louisville, Kentucky, on May 1, 1845. Amid increasing bitterness at northern treatment, the southern delegates quickly voted in favor of separation and of forming the Methodist Episcopal Church, South. They set up the structure for annual conferences and voted to hold their first official General Conference the following May in Petersburg, Virginia.

At the first General Conference, held in 1846, two bishops, William Capers and Robert Paine, were elected, and a series of publications established. The issue of boundaries was discussed but not resolved; this would be the subject of debate between the northern and southern Methodists for the next ten years. Most surprising of all was the declaration by Joseph Soule, that staunch New Englander, that he adhered to the southern church. Perhaps, in his mind, establishing a "connection" between the churches was more important than the moral issue of slavery. It was only in 1858 that the Methodist Episcopal Church, South, removed the ban against slavery from its Discipline; the North retained the rule.

By 1861 and the start of the Civil War, the lines of loyalty had already been drawn within the Methodist church—except in California. California had been missionized by both the Methodist Episcopal Church and the Methodist Episcopal Church, South, in 1849 and 1850. During the Civil War both churches existed amiably, far removed from the fighting, at one point even proposing a merger, which subsequently fell through because of mutual suspicion. In the rest of the church, however, the declaration of war produced predictable reactions. The northern Methodist Episcopal church backed the Union wholeheartedly, sending a statement of support to President Lincoln and, in 1860, strengthened their position by changing the rule banning slavery in the Discipline to a "New Chapter on Slavery." The northern church also participated in the United States Christian Commission, an interdenominational organization formed in 1861 to help the soldiers, and its ministers served as chaplains throughout the conflict.

The most controversial action of the northern church during the war was the seizure of churches in southern territories that had fallen to the North. This plan, organized by Bishop Edward R. Ames, garnered the support of Secretary of War Edwin Stanton. Stanton wrote the Union troops that, "You are hereby directed to place at the disposal of Rev. Bishop Ames all houses of worship belonging to the Methodist Episcopal Church, South, in which a loyal minister, who has been appointed by a loyal Bishop of said Church does not officiate." Lincoln limited this order somewhat, but it caused great bitterness in the South. At the war's end, the General Conference of 1864 was in a self-congratulatory mood: "The progress of the Federal arms has thrown open to the loyal Churches of the Union large and inviting fields of Christian enterprise and labor."

The Methodist Episcopal Church, South suffered greatly in the war, on the other hand. Initially advising patience and moderation, the church's leaders were, at last, forced to throw their lot in with the Confederacy. As if to atone, the southern church mounted an energetic mission among the slaves, although none of the church members advocated abolition. As in the North, southern ministers served as chaplains to the soldiers and worked to ease the suffering and devastation that swept their parishes. But, too, many fled their parishes as the northern troops advanced, leaving them up for grabs.

When the Civil War ended, the South and the Methodist Episcopal Church, South were in shambles. The churches had been destroyed or seized, their colleges closed, and ministers and congregations scattered or dead. The United States government had seized the church's Nashville printing office for federal purposes. Annual conferences could not meet, nor did the General Conference of 1862. Into this vacuum the northern Methodists came to "reconstruct" the church in the South. By 1869, there were ten northern conferences in the South, composed of 135,000 members served by 630 ministers. One of the most significant contributions that the northern Methodists made in the South, however, came through the formation of the Freedmen's Aid and Educational Society in Cincinnati in 1866. The Freedmen's Aid Society would become an official arm of the church in 1872.

Although the motives for founding the Freedmen's Aid Society, as it became known, were not entirely altruistic—the northern church saw it as a means of "retaking" the South—the effects were beneficial. The purposes of the society were to missionize and to bring education to the newly freed southern blacks. By the end of the first year, it had forty teachers and 3,000 students in nine states. The society established many schools and colleges, among which were Central Tennessee College in Nashville; Clark University in Atlanta; Rust College in Holly Springs, Mississippi; and

Meharry Medical College. While at first the mission was to aid blacks, it quickly came to include whites, Native Americans and, later, peoples in other countries.

The Methodist Episcopal Church was not the only northern Methodist church to missionize in the South at the end of the war. Previous to the Civil War and during it, black Methodists were forbidden to missionize in the South. Almost as soon as the Emancipation Proclaimation was signed, however, the black Methodist churches also started moving into the region. On April 27, 1863, the Reverend C. C. Leigh, a member of the Freedmen's Aid Society, attended the Baltimore Annual Conference of the African Methodist Episcopal Church and asked them to send two itinerant preachers south "as missionaries to care for the moral, social and religious interest of the freedmen in South Carolina, who were then as sheep without a shepherd, left in that condition by their former white pastors, who had fled before the advancing and conquering army of the Union." Enthusiastically, the conference voted to send James Lynch of the Baltimore conference and James D. S. Hall of the New York conference. On May 20, 1863, they sailed from New York to Charleston to begin their work.

On May 13, 1865, Bishop Daniel A. Payne, then head of the A.M.E. Church, came to Charleston to see the work that had been done by Hall and Lynch. It was a proud moment for Payne. Almost thirty years before he had been driven from that same city "for the crime of teaching colored children how to think and check." The following Monday, May 15, Bishop Payne officially organized the South Carolina Conference which included South Carolina, North Carolina, and Georgia. In the two years between 1863 and 1865, Lynch and Hall had converted 4,000 Methodists to the A.M.E. Church by their tireless, sometimes hazardous, hard work. In the eyes of the members of the conference, it was "like a ship sent to conquer other lands in the South."[3]

Black northern churches in the South had great success in missionizing, often for the same reasons as the northern Methodist Episcopal Church. Newly freed blacks distrusted, quite reasonably, the southern white preachers who had supported the system that had suppressed and abused them for so long. The black churches from the north had an additional advantage, however. Here were *black* preachers—something few southern blacks had seen before—coming to the southern black's aid. Many southern blacks were eager to disassociate themselves from anything that smacked of white control, and the idea of black ministers and bishops appealed to them greatly. By its second annual meeting, the South Carolina Conference was able to boast of a membership of between 48- and 50,000 souls, among which were a great many young men eager to join the ministry. At that session, fourteen applicants were accepted for the ministry and forty-six preachers were ordained deacons or elders.[4]

The A.M.E. Church faced competition in its drive for southern members, however. This came not only from the northern Methodist Episcopal Church but also from the equally zealous African Methodist Episcopal Zion Church and, after 1870, from the newly formed Colored Methodist Episcopal Church.

In 1863 Superintendent, later Bishop, J. J. Clinton was appointed to the Southern and Philadelphia Conference of the A.M.E.Z. Church. When first assigned to do southern work, Clinton hesitated to accept. The church did not have the funds to support such activity and he despaired of being able to do any good. While debating whether to resign the position or not, a Mrs. Melvina Fletcher from Washington, D.C., decided the matter for him:

> One memorable night, during the fall of 1863, she went to his stopping place, called him out of his sleep at 3 o'clock in the morning, and had the famous conference that changed his mind. When he complained that he had not a single minister or dollar to take a delegation as missionaries into the South, she remonstrated with him to tear up his resignation, promising that she would help raise the funds for his cause. Clinton needed $300, which she promised to raise. She went to her friends in the Blair orbit and the churches of Washington and raised it, and presented the $300 in gold to him as the fulfillment of her promise, to meet the need of the mission.[5]

Within a year Clinton had sent five preachers into the South: James W. Hood, Wilber B. Strong, John Williams, David Hill, and William F. Butler. Like the missionaries of the A.M.E. Church, the five met with resounding success in "receiving into Zion" southern blacks and, sometimes, whole congregations, frequently "stealing" them from the A.M.E. Church.

In 1864 Bishop Clinton traveled to North Carolina to organize the North Carolina Conference which included twelve ministers and four hundred members. James Hood, one of the missionaries sent by Clinton, wrote of his arrival, "Great was the joy of the people at being permitted to see a bishop of their own race, and especially a bishop who was willing to become all things to all men."[6]

The A.M.E.Z. Church rapidly spread throughout the South, from North Carolina to Florida, Tennessee to New Orleans, and into the West. By 1900, the A.M.E.Z. Church, like the A.M.E. Church, would span the continent, ministering to black Americans everywhere in the United States.

Both black Methodist churches, however, faced an indigenous competitor when they went south: the Colored Methodist Episcopal Church (renamed the Christian Methodist Episcopal Church in 1956). The C.M.E. Church arose from the unwillingness of the Methodist Episcopal Church, South to lose all its black members to the "carpetbagging" churches from the North, and from the recognition that those same black members did not wish to remain in white congregations in which they would be subjugated and segregated. They felt that a separate organization should be established with, however, strong and continuing ties to the Methodist Episcopal Church, South. Hence, in 1866 the idea of the Colored Methodist Episcopal Church was born:

> When the General Conference of 1866 asked, "What shall be done to promote the religious interests of the colored people?" that same body wisely resolved that "when two or more Annual Conferences shall be formed, let our bishop advise and assist them in organizing a separate General Conference jurisdiction for themselves, if they so desire and the bishops deem it expedient, in accordance with the doctrine and discipline of our Church, and bearing the same relation to the General Conference as the Annual Conferences bear to each other."[7]

On December 15, 1870, the first General Conference of the Colored Methodist Episcopal Church met in Jackson, Tennessee, presided over by Bishop Robert Paine of the Methodist Episcopal Church, South. It was attended by representatives of eight annual conferences that had been formed from black members throughout the South. They then organized a church against which, according to C. H. Phillips, the "gates of Hell should never prevail," drawing up a plan of organization and establishing a publishing house and fund-raising committees. William H. Miles and Richard H. Vanderhorst were elected and consecrated as the bishops and leaders of the C.M.E. Church.

Once the organizational structure was in place, the members of the C.M.E. Church immediately turned to the tasks of missionizing and winning those who had joined one or another of the northern churches that had been missionizing the South. The C.M.E. Church faced stiff competition. The northern churches charged that it was still in league with former slave owners and opposed to black advancement. While these charges were untrue, it was difficult to combat them because of the C.M.E. church's ties with the Methodist Episcopal Church, South. Yet the C.M.E. Church did progress. At the General Conference of 1873, it was reported that the C.M.E. Church had fourteen annual conferences, 635 itinerant preachers, 583 local preachers and a membership of 67,888.[8] By 1878, with a membership of over 100,000, the C.M.E. Church had become one of the fastest-growing Methodist churches.

All of the Methodist churches that were seeking new members in the South after the Civil War faced similar problems. Competition among them was fierce. In addition, there was confusion and argument over church and school properties. When a congregation moved from one church to another, to which did its property belong? Many of these disputes resulted in intense court battles, but equally often, protests were ignored, the new church simply taking over the property. As time passed, the arguments died down.

The South after the Civil War presented an opportunity for missionizing which no Christian church could ignore, although the Methodists, along with the Baptists, were in the forefront of the various denominations. This was in keeping with the energetic evangelism that was advocated by John Wesley himself. Methodists had been missionaries from the beginning, spreading around the world, into the American South and the American frontier. Where there was an opportunity, there usually were Methodist preachers. As the new century neared, however, the days of the itinerant preacher were coming to an end in America. Civilization was slowly crawling across the continent. As the 1800s turned into the 1900s, change was rampant in the United States, and that change would also be seen in the Methodist Church as a whole.

XII

Unity

AT THE SAME TIME THAT THE METHODIST CHURCH IN ALL its forms was combating slavery and missionizing in the United States, it was also embroiled in discussions confronting the philosophical and scientific issues of the day. Free will was pitted against determinism and eventually won out. The infallibility of the Bible was being contested and attempts were made to adjust biblical authority to modern trends in scientific and historical thought. Many were concerned about the "manifest loosening of the traditional bonds of popular respect for the Sabbath, the Bible, and the Church."[1]

Perhaps because the Methodists had always stressed education, their attitude toward the publication in 1859 of Charles Darwin's The Origin of Species was, for the most part, enlightened rather than condemnatory.

119

Instead of decrying its "blasphemous" ideas, most took the position of E. O. Haven, then president of Northwestern University. He maintained that the Bible was concerned with religion rather than matter: "So far, then, as the Darwinian hypothesis pertains to the origin of vegetables and animals or even man's physical structure, it is a matter of supreme indifference to Christianity."[2]

Also under debate at this time was the concept of "sanctification" of which John Wesley had written and spoken so often. Many liberals felt that the idea of original sin was untenable and that "the real cause of the first sin . . . is to be sought in the sinner himself." If there was no firm belief in original sin, there could be little interest in sanctification; those who espoused this view felt that man should strive for perfection, and that striving was a gradual and continuous process. On the other hand, those who had been caught up in the evangelism that swept the latter half of the nineteenth century, known as the Great Revival, felt sanctification to be a real and vital concept. Believers in original sin, these revivalists felt there was such a thing as an instantaneous cleansing of the soul through faith (similar to the "born again" experiences claimed by many fundamentalist Christians in the 1980s). As the revival fervor died down, there was a similar decline in interest about arguing the issue, however. Bishop J. F. Berry summed up the prevalent attitude when he said in 1896, "Don't you think we ought to stop debating about it now and begin to be holy?" What emerged was a more personal and less institutional view of sanctification: rather than follow a prescribed path, the individual could decide what was required to become sanctified.

The times were changing and Methodism was adapting to them. Many lamented this. At the Methodist Episcopal Church General Conference of 1900, while expressing hope for the new century and gratitude that the theological underpinnings of Methodism were unchanged, the bishops also noted:

> The class meeting, for instance, is considerably disused: have fellowship and spiritual helpfulness among believers abated, or do they find, in part, other expressions and other instruments? The rigid and minute Church discipline of former years is relaxed: is this a sign of pastoral unfaithfulness, or is it a sign of growing respect for individual liberty and of a better conception of the function of the Church? The plainness of the early Methodist congregations has disappeared.[3]

The new century meant change, but it also meant an opportunity to put aside old dissensions, old arguments; it heralded an age of cooperation. One of the first steps toward this cooperation occurred at the General Conference of 1900 when Frank Mason North and others called for a new commitment to social Christianity, a rededication to good works and the support of various social causes. His efforts bore fruit at the 1908 General Conference at which the Methodist Social Creed was adopted. This was to govern and shape the Methodist Church until the 1972 General Conference of the United Methodist Church, when an updated and more ecumenical social creed was adopted which read, in part,

> We believe in God, the Creator of humanity, the natural world, and society; and in Jesus Christ, the Redeemer of

creation. We believe in the Holy Spirit, through whom we receive God's gifts, and we repent of our sin in perverting those gifts to idolatrous ends. . . .

We commit ourselves to the rights of women, children, youth, and the aging; to improvement of the quality of life; and to the rights and dignity of ethnic and religious minorities.

We believe in the right and duty of persons to work for the good of themselves and others, and in the protection of their welfare in so doing; in the rights to property, collective bargaining, and responsible consumption; and in the elimination of economic and social distress.

We dedicate ourselves to peace throughout the world and to the rule of law among nations.[4]

Adopting a social creed was one thing, doing something about social ills, another. The Methodists set up new social programs and expanded others, missionizing around the world and contacting other denominations to help with the world's problems. A new era of ecumenicism was emerging.

The first indication that ecumenical ways of thinking were evolving came from a series of meetings held in London in 1881, which drew together representatives from most of the various Methodist churches. Out of these discussions came the formation of the Men and Religion Forward Movement, with the goal of achieving cooperation among the various Methodist churches. Later, in 1910, there was a further move towards cooperation with the first meeting of the World Missionary Conference. Here, different denominations exchanged ideas about missionary goals around the world. The spirit of ecumenicism didn't stop there, however, and eventually resulted in the founding of the World Council of Churches, an interdenominational body that promotes cooperation and understanding among the various faiths. The Methodist Church supported this ecumenical enterprise wholeheartedly, yet, ironically, as a body it was filled with splits and dissensions. The effort to heal itself began in 1929.

That year, representatives of the Methodist Protestant Church, which had broken away from the Methodist Episcopal Church during the heated debates over reform in 1828, approached Bishop Herbert Welsh to discuss the idea of reunification with the Methodist Episcopal Church and the Methodist Episcopal Church, South. A joint commission of representatives from the three churches was formed to study the proposal and to come up with a reunification plan. As negotiations progressed, all agreed that the resulting church, "The Methodist Church," would be governed through the office of Bishop, organized in a Council of Bishops. There would be one General Conference and six jurisdictional conferences, five of which would be geographical. A Judicial Council would be established as supreme arbiter of church law, and the Articles of Religion would be retained. The most difficult issue to resolve was what to do with the churches composed entirely of black members.

The attitudes toward the issue of blacks within the church illustrate what few opportunities had been given blacks after the Civil War. Although blacks were now free, segregation was the rule of the day. The northern churches, however, had an interest in maintaining black membership, while the South objected to any plan of reunification that included black church members. "It was the desire of this branch of Methodism to have the Negro in the northern branch set aside in a separate unit outside of the new united Church to be."[5] The committee finally decided that the sixth jurisdictional conference would be a non-geographical Central Jurisdiction, composed of the black members of the Methodist Church.

At the Methodist Episcopal Church General Conference of 1936, the black delegates expressed outrage at this segregation. When the matter was put to a vote, of the 47 black delegates, 36 voted against the plan and eleven abstained. Of the white delegates, however, 470 voted for and only 83 voted against. "It is reported that when the General Conference delegates arose, after the voting, to sing 'We Are Marching Upward to Zion,' the Negro delegates remained seated and some of them wept."[6]

As was to be expected, the Methodist Episcopal Church, South voted overwhelmingly for the plan at its General Conference in 1938 as had, earlier, the Methodist Protestants, and the union was formalized on April 26, 1939, in Kansas City, Missouri. As one black delegate, Dr. James Brawley, pointed out, there was great pride in the church itself, but deep regret "that the Methodist Church in the making had seen fit to write legal segregation into its constitution."[7]

In retrospect, it seems outrageous for a religious body to advocate the segregation of so many of its members. When the first General Conference of the Central Jurisdiction, the black jurisdiction, met in St. Louis, Missouri, in 1940, it was composed of nineteen annual conferences and 320,000 members.

This segregation would stand until 1956, when, in

the post–World War II wave of liberalism that would eventually lead to the civil rights marches of the 1960s, the General Conference of the Methodist Church adopted Amendment IX to its constitution. This permitted annual conferences to change from one jurisdiction to another if they wished, and also allowed local churches the right to switch annual conferences if the decision was unanimous. Later, in 1968, on the recommendation of a Commission on Inter-Jurisdictional Relations, the General Conference finally dissolved the Central Jurisdiction. The individual annual conferences of which it had been composed were now free to merge with existing white conferences and jurisdictions. After nearly thirty years, official discrimination against blacks was eliminated in the Methodist Church.

By 1960 there were 9,910,741 members within the Methodist Church. The church represented a union of disparate elements, yet there still existed fragmentation among Methodists. The three major black Methodist churches, the African Methodist Episcopal Church, the African Methodist Episcopal Zion Church, and what was now called the Christian Methodist Episcopal Church, remained separate. Jealous of their independence, these churches still refuse to unite with the Methodist Church or with each other. Yet, further unification was spurred from an unexpected quarter: the Evangelical United Brethren Church.

Philip William Otterbein, founder of the Church of the United Brethren, came to America in 1752. After preaching in a number of churches, in 1774 he assumed the pastorate of the German Evangelical Reformed Church of Baltimore. The congregation, like Otterbein himself, was strongly Pietist in orientation, emphasizing the Christian experience of salvation and the evidence of faith in daily activities. Otterbein was a strong believer in evangelism and this led to his encounter with Martin Boehm in 1767. The two met at a revival held in the barn of a Mennonite named Isaac Long, near Lancaster, Pennsylvania. Boehm was a Mennonite but had come to question the rigidity of Mennonite beliefs. Although a farmer, he had read extensively, particularly the works of John Wesley, and had taken to the spirit of evangelical revivalism then sweeping the country. Because of this, in 1775 the Mennonites excommunicated him.

After hearing Boehm preach, Otterbein went up to him and said, "Wir sind Brüder" (we are brothers), because Boehm seemed to echo so many of Otterbein's own thoughts on God and salvation. It was the beginning of a friendship that would last all their lives.

Otterbein's work as a minister in Baltimore, where there was a large Methodist community, led to a similar encounter with Francis Asbury. The two became fast friends and, in fact, William Otterbein was the man who ordained Francis Asbury in December of 1784, at his invitation. Asbury wrote of Otterbein, "There are few with whom I can find so much unity and freedom in conversation."

As the years passed, Otterbein and Boehm drew other ministers into their group and, in September of 1800 they met near Frederick, Maryland, to institute a series of annual conferences. The group was called the United Brethren and, like the early Methodists, did not constitute a denomination nor intend to become one. Both Otterbein and Boehm were chosen as *eltesten* (elders) with administrative authority over the group.

Despite Otterbein's death in 1813 and Boehm's in 1809, the movement which they had started seemed to have a life of its own. Itinerant preachers soon traveled the country spreading the ideas of the United Brotherhood in Christ, and more and more people sought to join. Denominationalism was almost a foregone conclusion and, in 1815, it became a reality. That year the first General Conference met in June to organize the group as a church, adopting a Discipline similar to the Methodists', with a similar outline of annual and general conferences. The two primary ways in which the United Brethren differed from the Methodists—which kept the groups from uniting until the twentieth century—was that bishops were elected for four-year terms, and both traveling and local preachers had voting rights at the annual conferences. The new church grew quickly, having a great deal of appeal to those of German descent. By 1890 the United Brethren had a membership of over 200,000.

While the United Brethren was evolving, nearby, also in Pennsylvania, another group was being formed. Jacob Albright was born in Montgomery County, Pennsylvania, in 1759, and was raised in the Lutheran Church. As a young man, saddened by the deaths of three of his children from dysentery, he heard a local Methodist preacher speak and converted to Methodism. By 1796 Albright was preaching himself, traveling throughout Pennsylvania and Maryland. By 1800 he had organized a number of small classes, independent of any church, and had garnered for himself quite a large following who wished to be united through him, rather than through any church.

In 1803 Albright met with a group of his followers in

Berks County, Pennsylvania. During the two-day meeting his group declared themselves a society under his direction:

> From the Elders and Brethren of His Society of Evangelical Friends: We the undersigned Evangelical and Christian friends, declare and recognize Jacob Albright as a genuine (Wahrhaftigen) Evangelical preacher in word and deed, and a believer in the Universal Christian Church and the communion of saints. Thus testify we as brethren and elders of his Society (Gemeinde).[8]

This meeting marked the beginning of the Evangelical Association (also known as Albright's People), which was formally established in 1816 at its first General Conference.

Unlike the United Brethren, the Evangelical Association clung to the German language and traditions until World War I. The Evangelical Association grew more slowly than did the United Brethren for this reason; by 1900 it had slightly over 166,000 members.

Members of the Evangelical Association did not see themselves as a "church," and many also belonged to the Methodist or the Lutheran churches, unwilling to depart from their upbringing. Yet it was, even from the start, becoming as much a church as had the United Brethren earlier.

Throughout the years, feelers had been put out by both groups about the idea of uniting, yet nothing happened until 1934. In that year, the Evangelical Association and the United Brethren organized a joint commission to study the matter and work on a plan for unification. In 1942 the General Conference of the

Evangelical Association approved the plan, 226 to 6. Three years later, the United Brethren General Conference also voted for the plan, 224 to 2. Both then submitted it to their annual conferences which approved it overwhelmingly. By 1946 the Evangelical United Brethren Church had been formed and was actively functioning.

In the ecumenical spirit that characterized the Methodist Church in the mid-twentieth century, the Evangelical United Brethren Church began discussion with them, also, about the possibility of a union. Initiated in the early 1960s, the discussions lasted the next eight years, with debates over authority and organization becoming heated at times. One issue that the Evangelical United Brethren Church insisted upon was racial desegregation of the Methodist Church and, by the time of the merger, on April 23, 1968, this had become a reality.

At the General Conference of 1968, held in Dallas, Texas, the United Methodist Church was born, bringing together 10,289,000 Methodists and 738,000 Evangelical United Brethren. One statement was repeated again and again at the conference: "Lord of the church, we are united in thee, in thy church, and in the United Methodist Church." The unity in Christ that John Wesley had envisioned so many years before was at last achieved for over eleven million people in the United States.

XIII

Modern Methodism

IN A 1980 GALLUP POLL, ONE IN EVERY THREE AMERICANS claimed to have been "born again," as a result of the Electronic Revival that swept the country in the wake of the free-wheeling sixties and the corruption of the seventies, as symbolized by the Watergate scandals.[1] Yet most experiencing a "rebirth in Christ" were doing so in the more fundamental denominations such as the Baptists and the Assemblies of God. Charismatics and pentacostals had gained in popularity and were heavily promoted by these sects. Miraculous healings and speaking in tongues provided hard evidence of God. The "me" generation that craved instant gratification in this world, also sought immediate relief and forgiveness for the next. One result of the increased popularity of fundamentalism was a loss of membership in the older Protestant churches, including the now firmly established United Methodist Church.

Ironically, the United Methodists, who could be said to have started the entire revivalist movement back in the 1700s, had by now abandoned the zealous emotionalism of their early days. They barely participated in the activities of the fundamentalist sects that proved so appealing to millions over the television.

Only the black Methodist churches—those that had never united with the other Methodist churches—benefited from the Electronic Revival. Never having eliminated the feeling, emotional side of spirituality, they spoke to more and more people, including young, educated blacks seeking a spiritual experience of their own in a white-dominated society. John Hurst Adams, senior bishop of the African Methodist Episcopal Church, said, "We are not buying the integration route. We never had and never will. We seek an inclusive society that need not be integrated but values diversity and respects it."[2]

Increasingly, American blacks were seeing in charismatics and pentacostalism a relief from their spiritual woes, and the black Methodist churches answered their needs with a resurgence of pentacostalism in their services. "The nerve center of black Neo-Pentacostalism is Bethel A.M.E. Church in Baltimore, which presents an invigorating blend of rollicking music and old-time religion. The church had 500 members in 1974; today [in 1990] it boasts more than 7,000. . . . Bethel is proudly Afrocentric."[3]

Yet the black Methodist churches face the same ills as society as a whole—homelessness, crime and drugs, perhaps the latter more so than the predominantly white churches. Drugs not only kill individuals and families, they also weaken the churches, drawing out their youngest members and destroying them. The answer has been more energetic social programs on the part of all denominations, but particularly within both black and white Methodism. Bethel Church, mentioned previously, in 1989 "clothed and fed 18,000 people, and it operates programs for older people, teens, women, youths with school problems and adults who cannot read."[4] In many ways, the latter part of the twentieth century, encumbered as it is by its multitudinous social problems, is ideal ground for the Methodist emphasis on "good works."

With the stock market crash of 1987 and the revelation of the corruption of leaders of various fundamentalist sects, membership in the United Methodist Church began again to climb. People were disillusioned by the quick-fix mentality of the late seventies and eighties, and sought something, spiritually, that was more solid and established. But solid did not mean stolid; people wanted their churches to be actively working against the ills of the times. They demanded that the Methodist church take a stance on such critical issues as racism, abortion, divorce, and the status of women. As usual, the United Methodist leaders had anticipated these demands.

In 1972 the United Methodist Church issued a list of Social Principles at its General Conference. On the subject of racism, they stated,

We reject racism in every form and affirm the ultimate and temporal worth of all persons. We rejoice in the gifts which particular ethnic histories and cultures

bring to our total life. We commend and encourage the
self-awareness of all ethnic minorities and oppressed
peoples which leads them to demand their just and
equal rights as members of society. We assert the obligation of society and groups within society to implement
compensatory programs that redress long-standing systematic social deprivation of ethnic minorities. We further assert the right of members of ethnic minorities to
equal opportunities in employment and promotion; to
education and training of the highest quality; to non-
discrimination in voting, in access to public accom-
modations, and in housing purchase or rental; and to
positions of leadership and power in all elements of our
life together.[5]

To implement this statement, the United Methodist
Church began numerous social programs, and expanded those already in existence, aiding ethnic minorities and the poor.

Likewise in the 1970s, the United Methodists formed
a commission on the role and status of women in the
church. Women had always played a very active role in
the church, teaching, running social programs, and
fund-raising, but, perhaps because of its patriarchal
origins, having been founded by John Wesley, women
had been excluded from leadership roles until the
twentieth century. Although women made up over 50
percent of the church, they did not have commensurate
power. During the latter half of the century, women
began demanding access to these positions, and suddenly more and more women were being ordained and
gaining an equal voice in the decision-making process
of the church. The modern United Methodist Church is
much more liberal than the rigid society envisioned by
John Wesley.

The church has also become more liberal in its attitude toward some of today's most crucial questions. On the issue of birth control, for example, the General Conference has stated,

> Parenthood is a Christian privilege and responsibility; and the highest ideals of the Christian family can be achieved when children are wanted, anticipated and welcomed into the home. We believe that planned parenthood practiced in Christian conscience fulfills rather than violates the will of God.[6]

The Methodist Church has worked to offer similar understanding to homosexuals, although it cannot condone homosexuality. The 1972 Social Principles state,

> Homosexuals no less than heterosexuals are persons of sacred worth, who need the ministry and guidance of the church in their struggles for human fulfillment, as well as the spiritual and emotional care of a fellowship which enables reconciling relationships with God, with others and with self. Further we insist that all persons are entitled to have their human and civil rights insured, though we do not condone the practice of homosexuality and consider this practice incompatible with Christian teaching.[7]

In implementing this principle, the United Methodist Church has instituted programs for homosexuals, and has worked to eliminate unfair laws and enact legislation that prohibits discrimination because of sexual orientation.

On the issue of abortion, the church has taken, again, an understanding stance. As Paul A. Washburn, who served as executive secretary of the union movement that resulted in the 1968 merger of the various Methodist churches, wrote,

> Our belief in the sanctity of unborn human life makes us reluctant to approve abortion. But we are equally bound to respect the sacredness of the life and well-being of the mother, for whom devastating damage may result from an unacceptable pregnancy. In continuity with past Christian teaching, we recognize tragic conflicts of life with life that may justify abortion. . . . We support removal of abortion from the criminal code, placing it instead under laws relating to other procedures of medical practice.[8]

The Methodists also maintain a compassionate attitude toward divorce. While recognizing and reaffirming the sanctity of marriage, the Methodists acknowledge the reality of human frailty and failure. However, the church only condones divorce on the grounds of adultery. If the breakdown is the result of some other cause, the couple is enjoined to seek counseling to remedy the marriage.

As the three hundredth anniversary of the birth of John Wesley approaches in 2003, the Methodists have much to look back upon and much of which they can be proud. From the small Holy Club of Oxford, Wesley's Methodists have expanded to cover the world through missions, hospitals, schools and universities, publications, and various social and reform movements. John Wesley avowed, "The world is my parish," and those who followed after him have made this vow a reality; in 1985, the Methodist denomination reached the twenty-four-million mark.[9] The call that Charles Wesley voiced in hymn has been heard by millions:

Sent by my Lord, on you I call;
The invitation is to all:
Come all the world; come sinner, thou
All things in Christ are ready now.[10]

Notes

Preface
1. Rupert E. Davies, *Methodism* (Harmondsworth, Middlesex, England: Penguin Books, 1963), 11.
2. Leo Rosten, ed., *Religions in America* (New York: Simon & Schuster, 1975), 179.

Chapter I
1. Rupert E. Davies, *Methodism*, 24.
2. John Pudney, *John Wesley and His World* (New York: Charles Scribner's Sons, 1978), 77–78.
3. Ibid.
4. R. K. Webb, *Modern England, From the 18th Century to the Present* (New York: Dodd, Mead & Co., 1968), 22.
5. Leo Rosten, ed., *Religions in America*, 100.
6. Anne Jordan & J. M. Stifle, *The Baptists* (New York: Hippocrene Books, 1990), 23.
7. John McManners, ed., *The Oxford Illustrated History of Christianity* (Oxford, England: Oxford University Press, 1990), 277.
8. Boris Ford, ed., *The Pelican Guide to English Literature*, vol. 4, *From Dryden to Johnson* (Baltimore: Penguin Books, 1966), 21.

Chapter II
1. John Pudney, *John Wesley and His World*, 7.
2. Ibid., 10.
3. Ibid., 12.
4. Ibid., 12–13.

Chapter III
1. John Pudney, *John Wesley and His World*, 14.
2. Ibid.
3. V. H. H. Green, *The Young Mr. Wesley* (London, England: Edward Arnold, 1961), Appendix I, 305–319.
4. Ibid., 20.

5. Frank Whaling, ed., *John and Charles Wesley*. (New York: Paulist Press, 1981), 9.

6. Ibid.

Chapter V

1. John McManners, ed., *The Oxford Illustrated History of Christianity*, 292.

2. Ibid.

3. John Pudney, *John Wesley and His World*, 55–56.

4. Frederick A. Norwood, *The Story of American Methodism* (Nashville: Abingdon Press, 1974), 34.

Chapter VI

1. Frederick A. Norwood, *The Story of American Methodism*, 47.

2. A. R. Humphreys, "The Social Setting," *The Pelican Guide to English Literature*, vol. 4, *From Dryden to Johnson*, ed. Boris Ford (Baltimore: Penguin Books, 1966), 42.

3. John Pudney, *John Wesley and His World*, 74.

Chapter VII

1. Frank Whaling, ed., *John and Charles Wesley*, 56.

Chapter VIII

1. Harry V. Richardson, *Dark Salvation: The Story of Methodism As It Developed Among Blacks in America* (Garden City, N.Y.: Doubleday, 1976), 37.

2. Frederick A. Norwood, *The Story of American Methodism*, 66.

3. Donald E. Byrne, Jr., *No Foot of Land: Folklore of Methodist Itinerants* (Metuchen, N.J.: The Scarecrow Press & The American Theological Assn., 1975), 206.

4. Robert Bull, "George Roberts' Reminiscences of Francis Asbury," *Methodist History* (5 July 1967), 28–29.

Chapter IX

1. As quoted in Frederick A. Norwood, *The Story of American Methodism*, p. 97.

2. Ibid., 99.

3. Ibid., 125.

4. Ibid., 176.

5. Ibid., 177.

Chapter X
1. Harry V. Richardson, *Dark Salvation*, 17.
2. Ibid., 9.
3. Ibid., 25.
4. J. F. Hurst, *The History of American Methodism* vol. 4, (New York: Eaton & Mains, 1903), 151.
5. Richard Allen, *Life, Experience and Gospel Labors* (Nashville: Abingdon Press, 1960), 27.

Chapter XI
1. Frederick A. Norwood, *The Story of American Methodism*, 197.
2. Ibid., 246.
3. Daniel A. Payne, *Recollections of Seventy Years* (New York: Arno Press and the *New York Times*), 470.
4. Harry V. Richardson, *Dark Salvation*, 196.
5. W. J. Walls, *The African Methodist Episcopal Zion Church, Reality of the Black Church* (Charlotte, N.C.: A.M.E. Zion Publishing House, 1974), 186.
6. As quoted in C. H. Philips, *History of the Colored Methodist Episcopal Church in America* (Jackson, Tenn.: C. M. E. Publishing House, 1898), 31.
7. Ibid., 24 ff.
8. Ibid., 58.

Chapter XII
1. As quoted in Frederick A. Norwood, *The Story of American Methodism*, 320.
2. Ibid., 322.
3. Ibid., 355–356.
4. Leo Rosten, ed., *Religions in America*, 183.
5. James P. Brawley, "Methodist Church From 1939," *Central Christian Advocate* (15 October 1967), 3.
6. Ibid., 4.
7. Ibid.
8. Frederick A. Norwood, *The Story of American Methodism*, 112.

Chapter XIII
1. Anne Jordan & J. M. Stifle, *The Baptists*, 149.
2. Richard N. Ostling, "Strains on the Heart," *Time* (November 19, 1990), 90.

3. Ibid.

4. Ibid.

5. As quoted in Leo Rosten, ed., *Religions in America*, 180.

6. Ibid., 177.

7. Ibid., 182.

8. Ibid., 181.

9. John McManners, ed., *The Oxford Illustrated History of Christianity*, 637.

10. As quoted in Frank Whaling, ed., *John and Charles Wesley*, 179.

Bibliography

Baker, Frank. *From Wesley to Asbury: Studies in Early American Methodism*. Durham, NC: Duke University Press, 1976.

Baker, George Claude, Jr. *An Introduction to the History of Early New England Methodism, 1789–1839*. New York: AMS Press, 1969.

Benson, Joseph. *An Apology for the People Called Methodists*. London: G. Story, 1801.

Bradley, David H. *A History of the A.M.E. Zion Church*, 2 vols. Nashville: Parthenon Press, 1956.

Carmen, Harry, et. al. *A History of the American People, Volume II—Since 1865*, 3rd ed. New York: Alfred A. Knopf, 1967.

Church, Thomas. *Remarks on the Rev. Mr. John Wesley's Last Journal. . . .* London: Printed for M. Cooper, 1745.

Clark, et. al. *Journals and Letters of Rev. Francis Asbury*. 3 vols. Nashville: Parthenon Press, 1958.

Davies, Rupert E. *Methodism*. Harmonsword, Middlesex, England: Penguin Books, 1963.

Emory, John, ed. *The Works of the Rev. John Wesley, A.M.* New York: John T. Waugh, 1835.

Fitchett, the Rev. W. H. *Wesley and His Century, A Study in Spiritual Forces*. London: Smith Elder & Co., 1906.

Ford, Boris, ed. *The Pelican Guide to English Literature, Volume 4: from Dryden to Johnson*. Baltimore: Penguin Books, 1966.

Frazier, E. Franklin & C. Eric Lincoln. *The Negro Church in America/ The Black Church Since Frazier*. New York: Schocken Books, 1974.

Hurst, J. F. *The History of American Methodism*. New York: Eaton & Mains, 1903.

Jordan, Anne Devereaux & J. M. Stifle. *The Baptists*. New York: Hippocrene Books, 1990.

McManners, John, ed. *The Oxford Illustrated History of Christianity*. Oxford, England: Oxford University Press, 1990.

Methodist Hymn Book. London: Methodist Conference Office, 1933.

Ostling, Richard N. "Strains on the Heart," *Time*, November 19, 1990, 88–90.

Payne, Daniel A. *Recollections of Seventy Years*. New York: Arno Press and The New York Times, 1968.

Perkins, David, ed. *English Romantic Writers*. New York: Harcourt, Brace & World, Inc., 1967.

Phillips, U. B. *American Negro Slavery*. New York: D. Appleton-Century, 1933.

Pudney, John. *John Wesley and His World*. New York: Charles Scribner's Sons, 1978.

Richardson, Harry V. *Dark Salvation: The Story of Methodism as It Developed Among Blacks in America*. Garden City, N.Y.: Doubleday, 1976.

Rosten, Leo, ed. *Religions of America*. New York: Simon & Schuster, 1975.

Southey, Robert. *The Life of Wesley*. Ed. J. A. Atkingson. London: Frederick Warne & Co., 1889.

Tyerman, L. *The Life and Times of the Rev. John Wesley, M.A.* London: Hodder & Stoughton, 1878.

Webb, R. K. *Modern England, From the 18th Century to the Present*. New York: Dodd, Mead & Co., 1969.

Wesley, Charles. *Journal*. 2 vols. Ed. T. Jackson. London: Matson, 1849.

Wesley, John. *A Christian Library. consisting of Extracts from and Abridgements of the Choicest Pieces of Practical Divinity, Which Have Been Publish'd in the English Tongue*. 50 vols. Bristol, England, 1749–1755.

———. *Journal*. Ed. N. Curnock. 8 vols. London: R. Culley, 1909–1916.

———. *Letters*. Ed. J. Telford. 8 vols. London: Epworth, 1931.

———. *Works*. 3rd. ed. Ed. T. Jackson. London: Mason, 1829–1831.

Whaling, Frank, ed. *John and Charles Wesley*. New York: Paulist Press, 1981.

Index